T0000752

Should All Drugs Be Legalized?

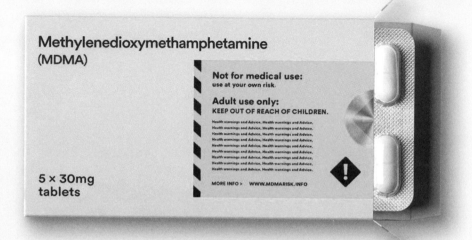

**Methylenedioxymethamphetamine
(MDMA)**

Not for medical use:
use at your own risk.

Adult use only:
KEEP OUT OF REACH OF CHILDREN.

Health warnings and Advice, Health warnings and Advice,
Health warnings and Advice, Health warnings and Advice,
Health warnings and Advice, Health warnings and Advice,
Health warnings and Advice, Health warnings and Advice,
Health warnings and Advice, Health warnings and Advice,
Health warnings and Advice, Health warnings and Advice,
Health warnings and Advice, Health warnings and Advice,
Health warnings and Advice, Health warnings and Advice,
Health warnings and Advice, Health warnings and Advice.

MORE INFO >   WWW.MDMARISK.INFO

5 × 30mg
tablets

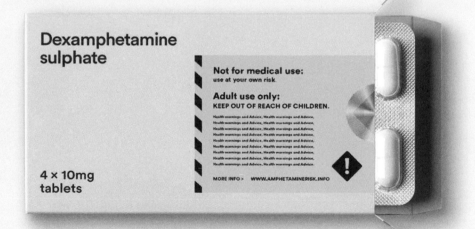

**Dexamphetamine
sulphate**

Not for medical use:
use at your own risk.

Adult use only:
KEEP OUT OF REACH OF CHILDREN.

Health warnings and Advice, Health warnings and Advice,
Health warnings and Advice, Health warnings and Advice,
Health warnings and Advice, Health warnings and Advice,
Health warnings and Advice, Health warnings and Advice,
Health warnings and Advice, Health warnings and Advice,
Health warnings and Advice, Health warnings and Advice,
Health warnings and Advice, Health warnings and Advice,
Health warnings and Advice, Health warnings and Advice,
Health warnings and Advice, Health warnings and Advice.

MORE INFO >   WWW.AMPHETAMINERISK.INFO

4 × 10mg
tablets

The Big Idea

Mattha Busby

Should All Drugs Be Legalized?

A primer for the 21st century

Over 200 illustrations

General Editor:
Matthew Taylor

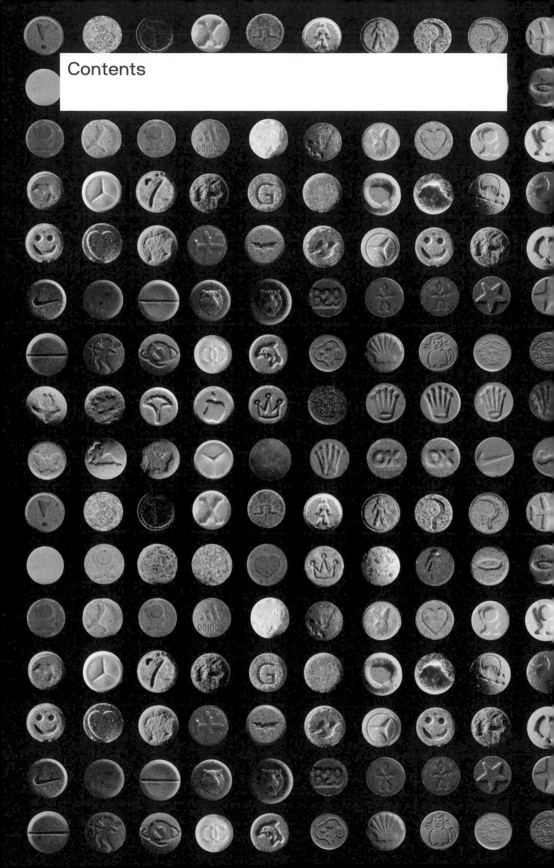

Contents

Introduction

A

There are few words in the English language that alone possess the capacity to shock. 'Drugs', a catch-all word accounting for medicines and intoxicants that have a stimulating, sedating or otherwise mind-altering effect, is one of them. Used judiciously, drugs can induce feelings ranging from ecstasy to serenity, relaxation and calm, while helping people to embrace spiritual and emotional intimacy.

Millions of people will attest to the best moments of their lives being experienced under the influence of some sort of drug. 'For everyday use there have always been chemical intoxicants,' writes Aldous Huxley in *The Doors of Perception* (1954). 'All these vegetable sedatives and narcotics, all the euphorics that grow on trees, the hallucinogens that ripen in berries...have been known and systemically used by human beings from time immemorial.'

Under the influence of many legal and illegal drugs, social situations become more fluid, flow states are reached and people better appreciate music, art, nature and sex. Our collective urge to explore altered states of consciousness is insatiable. We have long sought to improve our moods, relieve pain and enhance productivity; whether through sizeable consumption or microdoses. The desire to seek altered states seems universal, and a key UN body predicts that drug use will rise 11% by 2030.

A   Although sober 'ecstatic dances' are increasingly popular across the world, drug use and dancing have long been almost synonymous. Here young people dance at a nightclub in South Beach, Florida, USA.

B   Rather than taking an entire tab of LSD – an amount likely to induce an intense psychedelic trip – more and more people are regularly using minute amounts of a variety of hallucinogens to improve their mental health and productivity.

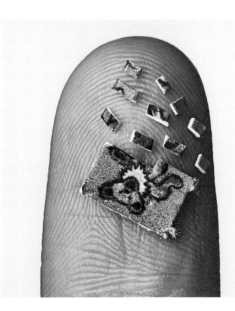

A

A   Paramedics treat a drug overdose victim on the pavement in a residential area of Washington, DC, 1993. Crack cocaine use surged in major cities in the USA from the late 1980s and through the 1990s. Cheap to produce and saleable in small quantities, the highly addictive drug became prevalent in low-income, inner city neighbourhoods that tend to have a large number of African American residents.

B   Troops in Thailand attempt to eradicate a poppy field in 1990 as part of a war on drugs policy. The campaign produced mixed results due to the sheer amount of land available for cultivation.

But there is a flipside. Particularly in ill-suited settings, both legal and illegal drugs are potentially dangerous and can be severely unpleasant – even lethal. A key question is, however, whether the drugs themselves cause most of the harm, or if the effects of prohibition – and current medical regulations – are even worse.

There were almost 500,000 recorded illegal drug-related deaths worldwide in 2019, including 167,000 overdoses – the death rate increased eight-fold between 1970 and 2006. More than 50 people per hour die from illegal drug-related deaths, and the rate is growing amid significant rises in major countries. However, the death toll from legal drugs, including alcohol and tobacco, is much higher.

B

Since the 1971 launch of the global war on drugs (the political manifestation of prohibition in its modern form), the harms associated with illegal drug-taking have risen steeply. It has become abundantly clear that mere laws do not stop human cravings, indeed it seems they often encourage higher-risk drug use by leaving supply in the hands of criminal groups. Contamination, unpredictable strengths, a lack of education and the encouragement of polydrug use by dealers wreak havoc. As well as their effects, the allure of illegal drugs is often underpinned by their forbidden fruit status.

A

From the outright legalization and regulation of cannabis to the decriminalization of drug possession and use, attitudes are gradually changing. In step with a growing acceptance that a number of illegal drugs have immense therapeutic value, some governments are slowly edging away from the historic failings of a war on drugs. Gradually, people are realizing that prohibitionist laws do more harm than the drugs themselves. The scale of the public health disaster appears to be horrific enough to countenance a radical new approach, but what would a world in which all drugs were legal look like?

We can infer some possibilities from existing legal drug markets, but it is hard to build a complete picture when so little has yet been tried, and the results would depend on the precise regulation model adopted. Sceptics point to the tobacco industry's disgraceful history and the US opioid crisis – effectively caused by pharmaceutical companies – as cause for any optimism to be carefully qualified.

Legalization removes prohibitions on the production, possession and use of drugs. Drugs may still be subject to regulations and controls, as with alcohol.

Regulation is the system of safeguards and rules governing the legal use and production of drugs.

Decriminalizion of drugs removes criminal sanctions for drug-related offences, often replaced by civil offences.

The opioid crisis has resulted from the prescription of highly addictive opioid medications in the US. Tens of thousands die annually as a result.

Pharmaceutical companies, or 'Big Pharma', produce and manufacture legal prescription and over-the-counter drugs for profit.

Alcohol, tobacco and addictive pharmaceutical drugs currently pose a greater real risk to humankind than illegal drugs. Alcoholism results in more than 3 million deaths each year, seven times the number of people who die each year from illegal drugs, while more than 7 million people die from smoking-related illnesses. Overall, smoking leads to the premature death of almost half of smokers. In excess of 500,000 people have died from prescription opioid painkiller overdoses in the US alone in the past two decades after an intense corporate advertising campaign that falsely suggested they were not addictive. In the US, prescription drugs are responsible for more deaths than illegal drugs, with significant numbers of people also dying from over-the-counter drugs such as paracetamol. This is almost certainly the case in a number of other countries, too.

A   As cannabis prohibitions around the world are relaxed, a diverse variety of weed-based products are emerging – from oils to edibles, creams and tonics – marketed as attractive consumables to mainly young white people.

B   The heads of the US' largest cigarette companies are shown being sworn into a hearing. In the 1990s more than 40 US states brought lawsuits against them, demanding compensation for the costs of treating smoking-related illnesses. 'Big Tobacco' settled in 1998 by agreeing to pay about $200 billion.

B

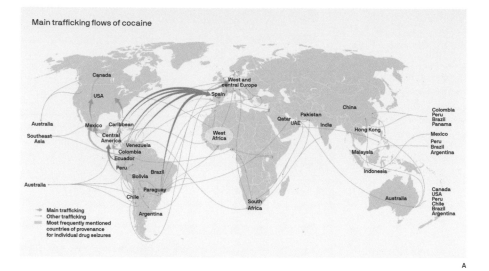

Main trafficking flows of cocaine

Canada
USA
Australia
Southeast Asia
Mexico
Caribbean
Central America
Venezuela
Colombia
Ecuador
Peru
Bolivia
Brazil
Australia
Paraguay
Chile
Argentina

West and central Europe
Spain
West Africa
Qatar
UAE
Pakistan
India
China
Hong Kong
Malaysia
Indonesia
South Africa
Australia

Colombia
Peru
Brazil
Panama

Mexico
Peru
Brazil
Argentina

Canada
USA
Peru
Chile
Brazil
Argentina

Main trafficking
Other trafficking
Most frequently mentioned countries of provenance for individual drug seizures

A

A   Coca leaves are grown exclusively in Latin America. They are transformed into cocaine using various chemicals in makeshift jungle laboratories and then exported across the world chiefly via Mexico and Spain.

B   Opiates are exported around the world from three main producing locations: Latin America, Myanmar and Lao PDR and Afghanistan.

However, in comparison to these industries, where production and supply are largely peaceful processes, the production and transit of illegal drugs carves a path of destruction and misery throughout many less developed countries and neighbourhoods. The US-led global war on drugs has failed to decrease global supplies while significantly eroding human rights, security, development and public health. In fact, US military actions have sometimes coincided with increased drug production and there have been a number of serious allegations implicating law enforcement and military forces in trafficking.

It is no coincidence that some of the most violent places in the world host key drug transit routes. In Colombia, cocaine sales fuel conflict; in Afghanistan, opium production – negligible before the Soviet and US invasions – has long bankrolled insurgents; in Mexico, cartels are often at war with each other if not the authorities, with whom they are sometimes embedded; and in several African states narco-money helps prop up kleptocracies.

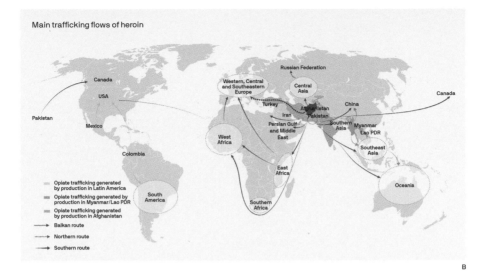

Main trafficking flows of heroin

Russian Federation

Canada

USA

Pakistan

Mexico

Colombia

Western, Central and Southeastern Europe

Central Asia

Turkey

Iran

Afghanistan
Pakistan

China

Southern Asia

Myanmar
Lao PDR

Canada

Persian Gulf and Middle East

West Africa

Southeast Asia

East Africa

Oceania

South America

Southern Africa

- Opiate trafficking generated by production in Latin America
- Opiate trafficking generated by production in Myanmar/Lao PDR
- Opiate trafficking generated by production in Afghanistan
- Balkan route
- Northern route
- Southern route

B

In the producer countries, where coca bushes, poppies and cannabis plants are grown, organized crime groups rule the countryside. Their power penetrates cities where politicians, police and business people are corrupted into protecting reputations and allowing the flow of drugs, while dirty money is laundered through mainstream institutions. Wars and nefarious activities are financed by the lucrative spoils of the drug trade. People who use drugs are often severely punished but those who profit the most rarely receive any serious comeuppance.

Cocaine is created from the coca leaf plant in South America, and is usually snorted or used to create smokeable crack.

Opium is traditionally grown in the Middle East. It is an intense relaxant that can be smoked and is also used to produce heroin.

Cannabis is the most ubiquitous illegal drug, with a variety of idiosyncratic subcultures attached to it. Weed generally makes users drowsy.

INTRODUCTION

15

A

In Juárez, northern Mexico, soldiers patrol the streets armed to the teeth. Fear is etched across the faces of many who walk past the ramshackle stores downtown, while sex workers stand outside dilapidated homes as gangsters watch on. The drug trade helped to transform the border city into a dystopian nightmare. Wars between cartels fighting over territory, amid concurrent pitched battles with state forces, have ravaged the surrounding region for much of the last 15 years. The city recovered from its war zone state in recent years after one group prevailed, but it remains extremely dangerous amid growing inequality and social exclusion. Women are kidnapped every week, with dozens dying every year, and whole neighbourhoods are enslaved by the drug gangs who collectively control an estimated 70% of the economy.

Could the situation be any different? No country has recently attempted to regulate any illegal drug besides cannabis for recreational use. If pragmatic regulation models that prioritized human rights and social justice were introduced, would violence related to drug markets across the producer and consumer countries of the Americas and Europe dramatically decrease? Is it possible that the profits and power of organized crime groups could be seriously undermined?

A number of jurisdictions have decriminalized the possession of drugs for personal use over the past two decades. In Portugal, the death and HIV infection rate fell rapidly as drugs were decriminalized in 2001 amid massive uptakes in treatment. The Czech Republic, which decriminalized drug use in 1989, withstood a potential crisis due to a robust treatment regime. Drug deaths now number in low double-digits. To the west, Switzerland rolled out a programme of prescribing medical-grade heroin to people with dependencies in the 1990s and it helped avert an extreme public health crisis.

Heroin is a highly addictive drug created from opium. Very pure forms may be snorted or smoked, whereas impure forms are injected.

A   Pink crosses erected in memory of eight women killed in Juárez, Mexico, in 2019. The city became infamous for the killing of women in the 1990s when hundreds were slain amid endemic masochism and growing drug-related violence.
B   Users inject heroin freely in the street in New Delhi, India, in 2006. Police are now taking a hard line in an attempt to eradicate the problem.
C   Syringes, plasters, dressing material and candles pictured in a legal drug consumption room in Frankfurt, Germany.

Across Europe, Canada and Australia there are now more than 150 safer Drug Consumption Rooms (DCRs) where people with dependencies can take illegal drugs in a hygienic, supervised space, and where there has never been a recorded fatal overdose. Elsewhere, many countries are adopting more pragmatic public health and harm reduction-led approaches, including providing the overdose antidote naloxone, offering diamorphine, providing drug safety testing, allowing registered people to access safe drugs from vending machines (as in Vancouver, Canada) and investing in early intervention addiction treatment schemes.

Would nothing short of a wholesale change in drug policies be necessary to significantly disrupt an illegal global market estimated to be worth in excess of $40 billion and that has infiltrated politics, big businesses and local high streets alike?

A

Drug Consumption Rooms (DRCs), also known as safer injecting facilities, are places where substances are consumed under safe supervision and wider support is offered.

Diamorphine is a version of heroin that is used in clinical settings. It is also prescribed to people with dependencies in some parts of the world to reduce harm.

Fentanyl is a highly potent synthetic opioid. Its strength makes it highly dangerous if not prescribed by a medical professional, or if it is combined with other drugs.

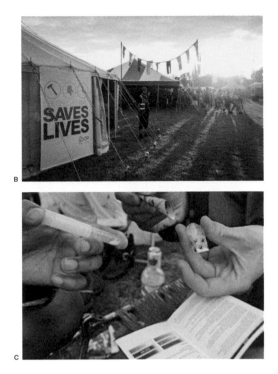

It seems that if you ban one drug, other new, more dangerous drugs will arrive on the market – look at how super-potent opioid fentanyl is emerging in the US heroin market – while drug contamination is also a serious issue that leaves many dead.

How did we get here? Did policymakers really think a drug-free world was possible? Why are some drugs legal while others remain prohibited? Finally, should all drugs be legalized?

1. Evolution of Drug Use and Production

A

A For millennia, Amazonian shamans have used drugs such as ayahuasca and DMT to interact with the natural world and God.
B A Greek terracotta bell-krater bowl for mixing wine and water from the mid-5th century BC. It depicts a symposium, the revels that took place after a banquet.
C An ornate Indonesian box (500 BC – AD 300) made to hold betel leaves. They have a mild stimulant effect and a number of health benefits.

Magic mushrooms contain the psychedelic psilocybin. 'Shrooms' were widely discovered in the mid-20th century and can make users hallucinate.

Humans have always explored altered states with drugs, whether for religious purposes, to numb pain and suffering, to prepare for battle or simply for pleasure to relax and socialize. Mention drug use to somebody today and it will most likely conjure images of cannabis smoking, cocaine snorting, heroin injecting or pill popping in clubs. But excessive alcohol drinking and tobacco smoking are embedded in cultures across the world, dependency on prescription drugs is growing and everyone knows a compulsive coffee or tea drinker. Today, it is difficult to think of many group occasions that do not at some stage revolve around some kind of mind-altering social lubricant – whether that be a caffeinated beverage, tobacco, alcohol, sugar or illegal drug.

Most drugs were either discovered by humans thousands of years ago or created by scientists relatively recently. We have indulged in alcohol, opium, cannabis and numerous other plant-based intoxicants since antiquity. Alcoholic drinks made from fermented grains, fruits and honey have been drunk for millennia. Beer was consumed 13,000 years ago in modern-day Israel, possibly for ceremonial use. Cannabis was most likely first cultivated 12,000 years ago in modern China. Rice wine was also drunk there up to 9,000 years ago and grapes have been fermented in Georgia for 8,000 years. Evidence of opium poppy cultivation has been found across Mediterranean Europe from the same period, with cannabis use also stretching back to that era in South Asia.

Ceremonies and religious rituals staged around the use of psychoactive plants have also occurred for thousands of years, allowing people to interrogate trauma and deepen their connection with nature. Recent evidence from North America suggests that hunter-gatherers were using tobacco around 12,300 years ago, and magic mushroom consumption may have originated 11,000 years ago. In parts of Latin America indigenous people have chewed coca leaves for about 8,000 years. San Pedro, the hallucinogenic cactus plant containing mescaline and used ceremonially for healing after coming-of-age pilgrimages, may well have been consumed in Peru more than 5,000 years ago; use of the psychedelic Amazonian healing brew ayahuasca is also thought to have begun then.

B   C

Traditional drug-taking was not seen as problematic until the violent arrival of colonists in Latin America and elsewhere. Modern consumption has a comparatively brief and chequered history.

Drug use has changed significantly over the past 50 years. We may have never seen before such mass legal and illegal drug use, no matter the deep historic roots of the human urge to get high. Unashamed and unabashed, illegal drug-taking in cities and villages the world over happens openly, privately and constantly. From prescription medicines to cocaine and cannabis, the use of drugs is at historically unprecedented rates, and has become normalized in many cultures. Most people know someone who uses illegal drugs all the time, or at least every weekend. Meanwhile, alcohol consumption and tobacco smoking has become less popular in some places.

As drugs have evolved (usually to increase profit and circumvent prohibitionist laws), so too have drug-taking behaviours. Cannabis originated in East Asia but is now cultivated in the vast majority of countries. Grown relatively easily almost anywhere (hence the nickname 'weed') on unmistakable green plants, it has long been used across the world and its portrayal as an evil drug is a recent phenomenon that has now almost entirely unravelled.

A

Bhang lassi is a yoghurt drink mixed with cannabis, traditionally drunk in India and associated with several religious festivals.

B

C

D

Whether drunk in a bhang lassi during the annual Holi festival in India, smoked as a sacrament for a Rastafarian ritual in Jamaica or puffed in Moroccan tea rooms, the use of cannabis is almost ubiquitous and has a remarkable ability to bring people together to create community.

A   Early 19th-century Indian painting showing the use of bhang. Made by grinding and soaking cannabis to form a paste, bhang has long been consumed in India, particularly at the Holi festival.

B   Poster for a US propaganda film from 1936, which vividly portrayed the unlikely effects of cannabis use. It even suggested cannabis could be injected intravenously.

C   Poster for a classic caper from 1936, which included a cannabis-fuelled hit-and-run accident, manslaughter, suicide, attempted rape and a decline into dependency.

D   Poster for a 1938 US film in which cannabis consumption leads to obscene and unpredictable all-night parties, echoing the fears of officials.

Cannabis has long been used to relieve malaria, constipation and rheumatism. The Vikings used it to ease toothache and help women during childbirth. Hashish (cannabis resin) was eaten in early Islamic states, and while those partial to it will have often done so in relative tranquillity, consumers in 14th-century Egypt were said to have had their teeth pulled out after the Ottoman ruler objected to its use, in one of the first cannabis bans in history. In 1787 it was banned in Madagascar, with its use punishable by death when the new king Andrianampoinimerina objected to people becoming 'half-witted'. Prohibitions followed in South Africa in the 1870s (solely for Indian immigrants), Mexico in 1920 and the US, in federal law, in 1937. This did little to stem its inexorable spread around the world and while the effect of cannabis use differs from person to person, prohibitions in the West are increasingly being abandoned or relaxed. In a famous routine in 1991, US comedian Bill Hicks (1961–94) commented, 'To make marijuana against the law is like saying that God made a mistake.' The UN deemed cannabis to possess no medical value and have 'particularly dangerous properties' in 1961, when it was strictly prohibited in response to US pressure. But the global body eventually downgraded cannabis in 2020 to permit research.

A

A A poster advertising 'Vin des Incas', painted by Alphonse Mucha in 1897, showing an Incan man paying tribute to a goddess seemingly representing coca. It is claimed that the potion helps convalescents.

B This set of prints, reproduced in 1882 from drawings made in 1850 by W. S. Sherwill, illustrates the opium production process at an East India Company factory in Patna, India. Crude opium arrived in the examining hall where it was chemically tested. It was then taken to the mixing room to be made into a paste. The mixed substance was then conveyed to the balling room and from there to the drying room. The balls were then stacked and turned before being conveyed by the opium fleet down the Ganges to Calcutta.

The *conquistadors* were the original Spanish invaders of Latin America who violently colonized vast swathes of the continent from the 16th century.

Similarly, a ban on coca – the plant from which cocaine is derived – was abandoned once its unenforceability in Latin America was realized by the *conquistadors*, who had swiftly attempted to eradicate its use. The Incan government had a monopoly on it and only permitted coca use during rituals or for certain workers as it was considered sacred and lauded for its ability to energize, suppress appetites and mask fatigue. Initially branded 'an evil agent of the devil', it was made widely available and taxed after the Spanish noticed that workers struggled to harvest crops and mine for minerals in its absence. This precipitated a rapid spread in its use: in the words of writer Eduardo Galeano, the *conquistadors* 'energetically stimulated its consumption'. The Catholic Church entered the business, and hundreds of white merchants in Cuzco, in modern-day Peru, lived off the industry.

Around three centuries later, when US pharmaceutical companies began to explore the region for new medicines, coca swiftly entered the Western pharmacopeia in tonics to ease pain, pills to prevent nausea and drops for toothache. Its quick numbing qualities saw it touted as a medical miracle and Pope Leo XIII (1810–1903) awarded French chemist Angelo Mariani (1838–1914), creator of a popular coca wine, with a gold medal and appeared on an endorsement poster.

It, and similar products, were aggressively marketed – even at children and the elderly, for whom it was advertised as an instantaneous pain cure and an aphrodisiac superior to any other drug. However, the side effects and its addictiveness were then widely unknown due to a lack of testing. Then, in 1859, German chemist Albert Niemann (1834–61) isolated cocaine from exported coca leaves. It was on its way to becoming the world's chic drug, reportedly used by everyone from Sigmund Freud (1856–1939) and Émile Zola (1840–1902) to Queen Victoria (1819–1901) and Ulysses S. Grant (1822–85).

Opium was also immensely popular during this era. Its known use stretches back thousands of years across Iraq and Syria, where it was referred to as *hul gil*, the 'joy plant'. The Sumerians, Assyrians, Egyptians, Greeks and Romans would all later use it too, with the writer Homer (b. *c.* 750 BC) noting it lulled 'all pain and anger' and brought 'forgetfulness of every sorrow'. Cultivation soon spread swiftly along mountainous parts of the Silk Road trading route – from China to the Mediterranean – in the 15th century.

B

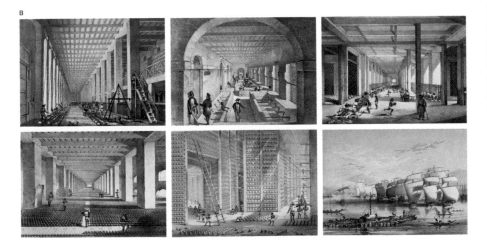

A   Chinese Americans photographed in an opium den (1890–1910). US media at the time focused on the consumption of opium by Asian people, despite use by white people not being uncommon.

B   Photos of seized opium consumption equipment published by the US Treasury in 1919 in an attempt to emphasize a crackdown.

C   A disgruntled saloon keeper laments that he cannot compete with the drug trade in this 1900 illustration featured in *Puck*. Opposite him, a crowd of eager consumers line up at the pharmacy, seeking arsenic, nerve stimulant, opium and cocaine.

Paracetamol is a popular over-the-counter medicine that helps relieve the symptoms of fevers and pain but has side effects of nausea and abdominal pain. It faces increasing regulatory scrutiny.

Opium smoking became increasingly popular in Imperial China in the late 16th century, although it had been consumed medically for 800 years. The country was exploited by aggressive British opium pushing that culminated in the sacking of Beijing when Chinese authorities eventually strenuously objected. In Victorian Britain, tinctures containing the natural drug, such as laudanum, were used extensively by adults and children for insomnia, melancholia, heart problems and cholera.

Available over the counter at pharmacies, all manner of drugs were laced with morphine and opium to alleviate mild and chronic symptoms. It was the paracetamol of the era. Though it cured few ailments, doctors felt as though they had been handed a magic wand since it could both relieve and anaesthetize with ease. Untaxed, poorer people also consumed it to relax, even adding it to beer, because it was cheaper than gin or wine. Its use was both rife and unrestricted – in the UK at least – until 1868.

Like opium, public opinion turned against cocaine once the stimulant's addictive and destructive qualities became clear. The manufacturers of Coca-Cola – which contained a small line of cocaine in each bottle and was marketed as 'an intellectual beverage... offering the virtues of coca without the vices of alcohol' – removed coca from the drink in 1904 (though it remains flavoured by part of the leaf) before it was outlawed a decade later.

Yet, like bootlegged liquor during America's catastrophic experiment with prohibiting alcohol, demand did not disappear. In the UK and elsewhere cocaine had been accessible in pharmacies for decades and, after World War I, it spread across Europe, becoming particularly popular in Germany and Russia.

c

THE AGE OF DRUGS.

Suddenly, in the 1960s, there was a resurgence of use and within two decades 6 million Americans were using cocaine regularly, with the drug somewhat glorified in movies and wider popular culture even as its risks became more widely known. Once the preserve of the wealthy and famous, falling global prices in the 1980s led everyone from bankers to manual workers to indulge in and abuse it.

Amid the plummeting prices, backstreet chemists and drug dealers discovered cocaine could be cooked into crack. The rocks could be consumed more swiftly through smoking, creating an intenser yet shorter-lived high. Its use – largely by poorer people – has often been closely associated with the illegal heroin trade, where dealers found a ready market for a drug that offers a different form of escape.

A

B

c

A First published in
1976, when cocaine
was at its most
socially acceptable,
this book sketches
the drug's history
and explains how
to ascertain its purity.
B In the 1970s
legitimate companies
manufactured
paraphernalia to aid
cocaine consumption,
such as an ivory
'ideal coke surface'.
C Revellers on the
dancefloor at the
legendary Hacienda
club in Manchester
in 1988, possibly
under the influence
of MDMA.

In Latin America, indigenous people continue to chew coca in much the same way as they and their ancestors have always done, without mixing the leaves with the gasoline, cement and sulphuric acid used in makeshift jungle laboratories to make cocaine.

Today, an estimated 21 million people use MDMA (or 'ecstasy') each year. It was created by Merck in the 1910s before a version of it initially sidestepped global prohibition due to its deliberate chemical structure decades later. MDMA usually comes in the form of a pill that can create a sense of euphoria and emotional empathy and which first became popular across Europe in the late 1980s during the golden age of the house, techno and rave electronic music scenes. Ecstasy characterized the emergence of rave culture and encouraged radical, utopian views.

Crack is a smokeable form of cocaine. It appears as rocks and is created with the help of baking soda. It brings a more intense high and sudden side effects.

Jungle laboratories are makeshift facilities, mostly near to coca fields, where the plant is mixed with petrol and other chemicals to produce cocaine.

MDMA, also known as molly and in tablet form as ecstasy, brings waves of euphoria by speeding through the body's serotonin, the happiness chemical.

A One struggles to imagine a legal ecstasy market that would be allowed to market the drug as candy, although this is how it is foolishly treated by some.

B Dr Harry Williams squirts LSD from a syringe into the mouth of Dr Carl Pfeiffer. Pfeiffer used the drug to perform experiments in behaviour control in prisons for the CIA from 1955.

C A volunteer takes LSD for a research project in Viejas, California, in the 1960s. Such projects were beginning to indicate that 'acid' could have useful mental health effects before research was stymied for political reasons.

A

PMA is an amphetamine similar to MDMA, but with more toxic effects that take longer to kick in, making it easier to overdose.

LSD, also known as acid, is a powerful hallucinogenic drug. It may be taken as a liquid or a tab. The hallucinations, or trips, experienced by users are normally enjoyable but can be distressing.

From raves in Ibiza to the world beyond, the strength of MDMA, also known as molly, is growing. The pills increasingly adopt popular culture symbols or the corporate logos of Facebook, Donkey Kong, Skype, Tesla and Louis Vuitton, in a direct appeal to younger people. Although there is little risk of dependency, dangerously high-strength pills can lead people to unwittingly fatal overdoses. Sometimes cut with PMA – which can trigger psychotic episodes and has a slower onset than MDMA – many soon discover what they have taken is not what they thought it was as they trip out and experience unpleasant effects such as anxiety or insomnia, or may need to visit hospital. Frustratingly for some, the effect of the drug rapidly declines with frequent use.

Much like MDMA's inadvertent originators, who patented it as a diet pill, chemist Albert Hofmann (1906–2008) did not intend to create a psychedelic drug during the 1930s. After accidentally absorbing a small amount he fell into a dream-like state and 'perceived an uninterrupted stream of fantastic pictures, extraordinary shapes with intense, kaleidoscopic play of colours'. By 1947, LSD had been introduced as a medicine for psychiatric uses under the proprietary name Delysid.

LSD use became popular in the 1960s after psychiatrists began testing it themselves and sharing it with their friends. It was used to enhance the creativity of artists and composers and by a growing group of people interested in exploring states of altered and expanded consciousness. Psychedelic images reimagining the hallucinations or visions experienced when on LSD entered the mainstream. The experience became much loved by disparate cross sections of society, mainly in North America and Europe. Ken Kesey, author of *One Flew Over the Cuckoo's Nest*, said LSD seems 'to give you more observation and insight, and [makes] you question things you [do not] ordinarily question'. It is neither habit-forming nor associated with fatal overdoses.

B
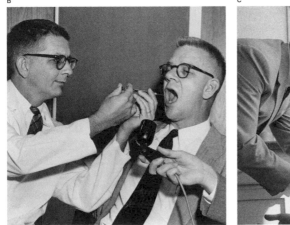

C
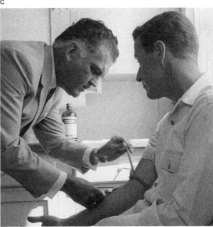

A   Psilocybin truffles, most commonly sold legally in Amsterdam, Netherlands, have a bitter flavour and carry a fizzy effect that may lead consumers to feel sick, while enjoying an intense high and possible hallucinations.

B   Liberty caps, the psychedelic mushrooms found across Europe and North America, usually grow next to dung. The fruiting season has extended in recent years due to climatic changes.

C   Microdosing psilocybin mushrooms has become increasingly popular as an alternative therapy, both to increase productivity and focus and to ease mental health issues among those who do not wish to take pharmaceutical drugs.

D   Tech workers on America's West Coast have been at the forefront of the growing use of LSD microdoses – such as the fractions of a tab shown here.

Other psychedelic drugs grow naturally in plants and fungi. Humans first began eating 'magic' mushrooms in Mexico and Siberia thousands of years ago, but their more widespread use has curiously been confined to the last 50 years in most countries. Now, use of 'shrooms', which contain the active ingredient psilocybin, is increasing, as people discover the plants that sprout spontaneously from our soil.

There are far more 'shroomers' today than ever before in history, and mushrooms are grown across the world, to fuel Full Moon Parties in Thailand and hallucinogenic treks in the US. A wider psychedelic movement is nascent. Ceremonies increasingly take place in Western cities, by self-taught shamans and those who have studied with elders. Clinical trials are indicating psilocybin could revolutionize the treatment of a whole host of medicine-resistant conditions, and strict regulations on medical use and research are slowly being relaxed.

A

B

Full Moon Parties are infamous free-spirited fiestas on beaches in Thailand, with many under the influence of magic mushrooms.

Esketamine is made from ketamine, and is now being used as a groundbreaking therapy to provide relief from serious depression.

Microdosing is the practice of regularly taking small amounts of psychedelics at a dosage where psychoactive effects are not overtly perceivable to boost creativity, productivity or problem-solving ability.

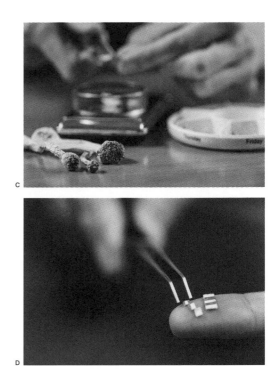

C

D

Ketamine, developed in 1962, has recently been approved for use on people with depression. A 'dissociative anaesthesia' long used in clinical settings around the world, ketamine can quickly sedate and relieve pain – and induce hallucinations and out-of-body experiences distinct from classic psychedelics – while maintaining cardiorespiratory stability. It soon became popular as a useful anaesthetic for emergency medicine (including in military scenarios) and for vulnerable populations, such as children and the elderly. It also became increasingly sought after for non-medical use in the late 1970s.

In 2013 the US Food and Drug Administration gave esketamine – which can return the brain to child-like capacities for learning – Breakthrough Therapy designation. Specialist clinics are opening and the drug is increasingly being prescribed for mental health conditions. Similar effects can be gained from psychedelic plants, including ayahuasca, ibogaine, peyote and psilocybin. A growing body of evidence indicates they have the capacity to reboot the brain and address the symptoms of emotional and mental issues. Microdosing has also become more popular, notably in Silicon Valley.

A A shaman in Yarinacocha, Peru, facilitates an ayahuasca ceremony with villagers in 2018.

B Peyote is a psychedelic succulent, native to Mexico and southwestern Texas. It is considered sacred by the Huichol – who believe it grows in the footprints of deer – and they undergo pilgrimages based around the harvest.

C The potent crown or 'button' of the mescaline-containing peyote cactus should be sliced diagonally above the root to allow it to continue to grow.

Ayahuasca is being used therapeutically, though usually not legally. Evidence is growing of a wide range of positive effects on mental health as normally dormant parts of the brain communicate with each other to facilitate more positive thinking. People report connecting with dead loved ones and even communing with a nature goddess, while unearthing and addressing past traumas. Indigenous communities have used the mixture of plants for around 5,000 years, according to some scholars, and ayahuasca rituals are a spiritual bedrock for tribes in the Amazon who gain wisdom from *madre ayahuasca*. In the US, since a court ruling in 2009, its use has been permitted within religious settings, as in Brazil since 1992. The brew, like others, is increasingly touted by those who have experienced it as a potential salve for humanity.

In northern Mexico, indigenous people have harvested peyote – an inconspicuous cactus containing the psychedelic drug mescaline – each year from the desert since as far back as 10,000 years ago. It can be chewed, cooked or its powder extracted, and can also be found in the southwest of the USA along with the similar San Pedro. During the Spanish conquest of Latin America in the 16th century, the invaders attempted to convince the indigenous people that peyote was evil and associated with communion with the devil. Peyote has long been used mainly for religious purposes to trigger states of spiritual introspection and remains largely tolerated in these settings, notably being legal in the USA for certain sacramental uses since 1994.

Reminiscent of the *conquistadors*' attempts after they arrived in Latin America, plant-based psychedelics nevertheless continue to be wantonly demonized and associated with evil in many places. In a culture awash with drug misuse, prescription chemicals and mood-altering antidepressants, writes Daniel Pinchbeck in his foreword to *The Psychedelic Experience* (2017), it seems strange to prevent the use of natural medicines. Perhaps there are fears that greater psychedelic drug use could increase pressure on the establishment to make radical reforms. After all, they are certainly seen as a threat to religious, cultural and institutional medical norms.

B   C

BARACK OBAMA
President, USA
2009–2017

'Pot had helped, and booze; maybe a little blow when you could afford it... I inhaled frequently. That was the point.'

DAVID CAMERON
Prime Minister, UK
2010–2016

'I did lots of things before I came into politics which I shouldn't have done. We all did.'

DONALD TUSK
President of the European Council
2014–2019

'Life in workers hostels does not favour reading Plato. These were not sanctuaries and we were not angels.'

A

A/B Entitled 'Politicians Take Drugs Too', this set of playing cards was created by the drugs charity Release. Many politicians have admitted to drug use, perhaps in some cases in an effort to relate better to voters.

Why do we vilify people who use certain drugs in certain ways? Those who have fallen victim to the dependency-forming capacity of a drug are dismissed as 'junkies', 'fiends', 'users' and 'addicts' – stigmatizing words that have been proven to negatively alter how healthcare professionals approach patients.

But as with alcohol, the majority of people who take drugs do not use them problematically. To challenge stigma, the charity Release produced the campaign slogan 'nice people take drugs'. It was displayed on the sides of buses in the UK until the Committee of Advertising Practice forced the charity to take it down in June 2009.

The globalization of legal and illegal drugs as commodities in an emerging capitalist marketplace, beginning in the 17th century, was a profit-motivated process. Alcohol, tobacco and caffeinated products became ingrained in the culture of the dominant colonial elites and were thus largely impervious to prohibition, but opium, cannabis and coca remained comparatively exotic, more easily associated with an 'other'. As the state sought to play a larger role in people's lives in the post-war period, these 'other drugs' were prohibited globally.

Since then, they have nonetheless proliferated alongside a growing pharmacopeia of easily manufactured synthetic drugs often designed to circumvent laws prohibiting the use of existing drugs.

2. Effects on Individual and Social Health

A

Sprawled across pavements in London, hunched in doorways in New York, slouched in crack houses in Rio de Janeiro and hidden under bridges in Johannesburg, the public face of drug use – commonly recycled in the media and public discourse – is overwhelmingly a negative portrayal of the most problematic end of the drug-use spectrum. This perception is etched into public consciousness far more vividly than that of the drunk stumbling along the pavement, which is often regarded as funny rather than feared. Meanwhile, millions remain behind closed doors, surreptitiously and pleasantly indulging in their vices without eliciting negative attention.

Still, for the last half century or longer, drugs have been treated as a scourge, and dependency an issue of morality. Reformers say that it would be sensible to educate people about safer use, rather than sending them to prison, where harm-reduction measures may be even less accessible and drugs could be far easier to procure.

Millions of people have died directly as a result of drug use in recent years. Around 35 million people globally have drug use disorders and require treatment services, about a tenth of the estimated 340 million people who use drugs at least once a year. That is just over 1 in 20 people in the world, and the figure has increased by almost a third over the past decade. But people who use drugs are not just cocaine snorters, cannabis smokers or heroin injectors. Many use them consciously for healing.

Meanwhile, potentially dangerous medicines – often including otherwise prohibited drugs, such as benzodiazepines and steroids – are over-prescribed and doctors may give drugs solely to manage symptoms, rather than suggest holistic, wraparound solutions geared to cure.

A   A man slumps against a wall in the South Bronx, New York City, June 2017. Drug use, especially heroin and other opioids, has exploded on the streets of the US in recent years. In 2017 overdoses became the leading cause of death for Americans under the age of 50.
B   Drugs available on prescription at a pharmacy in London. All manner of potentially harmful, yet also beneficial, drugs are sold legally in pharmacies. Around one third of US-approved drugs have serious safety issues and many are subsequently withdrawn.
C   Drunken spectators, one of whom wears an 'I ♥ COKE' shirt, congregate for the UEFA Euro 2020 Championship final between Italy and England, July 2021. Cocaine use at football matches is increasing in the UK.

The specific legal status of drugs is often arbitrary, based on historical and political anomalies such as racist assumptions and corporate pressure. Lawmakers and doctors came under sustained pressure from corporate producers in the US in recent decades to prescribe opioid painkillers, the addictiveness of which was concealed. Driven by the illegal market, hundreds of thousands have died, after profit-driven over-prescribing also helped create a generation of middle-aged people hooked on potent legal drugs.

Society is evidently not opposed in principle to people experiencing altered states of consciousness. Alcohol is glorified; tobacco is smoked recklessly in many places; tea and coffee are drunk all day along with extremely unhealthy energy drinks; and high levels of sugar are in many, if not most, processed foods. If you are accustomed to them, try to go without one of these drugs for a decent period of time, and you will realize the scale of your dependency. These are 'approved' altered states of consciousness that do not pose any perceived threat to society or the economy. In fact, they may help you get through your day, whether you are working in business, construction or science.

A

B

A   Activists from Prescription Addiction Intervention Now (PAIN) stage a 'die-in' outside the US bankruptcy court in White Plains, New York, in 2021, calling for the billionaire Sackler family to face justice over their key role in one of the worst public health scandals in US history: the opioid crisis.
B   One of the thousands of 'Oxy Dollars' and prescription bottles of OxyContin thrown by PAIN activists outside the courthouse in White Plains as they call for harm-reduction funding.
C   Deaths as a result of illegal drug use are dwarfed by those resulting from diet-related illness, car accidents and alcohol.

Coffee is described as the world's silent addiction. The caffeine it contains makes consumers more alert but also causes withdrawal symptoms such as headaches and severe irritability.

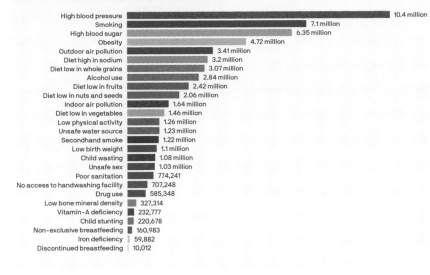

Number of deaths worldwide by risk factor (2017)

High blood pressure	10.4 million
Smoking	7.1 million
High blood sugar	6.35 million
Obesity	4.72 million
Outdoor air pollution	3.41 million
Diet high in sodium	3.2 million
Diet low in whole grains	3.07 million
Alcohol use	2.84 million
Diet low in fruits	2.42 million
Diet low in nuts and seeds	2.06 million
Indoor air pollution	1.64 million
Diet low in vegetables	1.46 million
Low physical activity	1.26 million
Unsafe water source	1.23 million
Secondhand smoke	1.22 million
Low birth weight	1.1 million
Child wasting	1.08 million
Unsafe sex	1.03 million
Poor sanitation	774,241
No access to handwashing facility	707,248
Drug use	585,348
Low bone mineral density	327,314
Vitamin-A deficiency	232,777
Child stunting	220,678
Non-exclusive breastfeeding	160,983
Iron deficiency	59,882
Discontinued breastfeeding	10,012

C

Prohibitions of illegal drugs are maintained ostensibly due to the perceived harms the drugs pose, with policymakers wilfully ignorant of the collateral damage of prohibition. Some might argue that prohibition is seen as a means of preserving the ways of our established, mostly heteronormative, patriarchal and racist world obsessed with social control.

Most things in life have an element of risk, from driving, eating and drinking to undergoing operations. More than 1.25 million people around the world die every year following road traffic accidents, while up to 50 million others suffer non-fatal injuries. Road traffic accidents, not drugs, are the leading cause of death among people aged between 15 and 29. Amid an omnipresence of fast-food restaurants located prominently on high streets and business parks to serve the ingredients for chronic disease within moments, poor diet is also a major contributor to misery. Obesity and lacklustre diets contribute to millions of deaths a year from diabetes, liver disease and high blood pressure. So why do we not ban fast food? Some enjoy it occasionally, others overdo it. Like drugs.

A

B

Cannabis is the illegal drug that people around the world are most likely to have consumed. One in 25 people worldwide use cannabis, and this may well be a conservative estimate. Most people can enjoy moderate cannabis use with no ill effects. Many claim there has never been a recorded death solely attributed to cannabis, though it is contested. You simply cannot overdose on the stuff and, unlike most drugs and prescribed pain medications, it has a number of health benefits, though smoking poses dangers, as does heavy use particularly among younger and vulnerable people – especially as the strength of products in some places has almost quadrupled since 1995 as dealers seek to maximize profits.

The laws restricting the use of cannabis are ignored to various degrees. This is visibly demonstrated by the 4/20 annual cannabis celebrations, at which people who use it take to public places to light up en masse. It has only become controversial relatively recently, given its long history of use.

Many people who use cannabis will have a story of taking too much and experiencing negative effects. The unwanted effects can include paranoia, anxiety, panic attacks and impaired short-term memory; it can also trigger serious mental health episodes in people with pre-existing conditions, such as schizophrenia and psychosis. Particularly frequent use of the high-strength varieties heightens the risk of these unwanted effects, and it can also be habit forming.

Cannabis-based medicines are now being prescribed across more than 50 countries that have legalized it for medicinal purposes, though resistance to prescribing remains in medical establishments and patients often risk arrest for obtaining their medicine through the illegal market. People with epilepsy, multiple sclerosis, Crohn's disease, chronic pain, anorexia and cancer report positive, sometimes life-saving effects from a range of cannabis-based medicines, including both the psychoactive component that makes you high – THC – and the non-psychoactive agent, CBD.

A   A South African cannabis grower takes a break from harvesting his new crop in March 2020.
B   A cannabis activist holds a flag aloft during the US annual Independence Day march in 2021, calling for the freedom to smoke the plant.
C   *The Simpsons* character Homer Simpson is depicted suffering from the effects of cannabis misuse in graffiti art in Freetown Christiania, a hippy commune in Copenhagen, Denmark, famed for its open cannabis trade.

Schizophrenia is a mental health condition and form of psychosis. Sufferers experience distortions in thinking, perception, emotions, language and behaviour.

Psychosis is experienced when people lose some contact with reality. This may involve experiencing hallucinations or delusions.

C

The tail winds of drug policy reform are cannabis-infused, and many people see the liberalization of cannabis laws as opening up space for debate around more far-reaching reforms regarding other drugs. The degree to which these changes are, in places, driven by commercial, profit-seeking corporate forces, however, has disappointed social justice campaigners. Flashy billboards advertising cannabis in parts of the US may be a glimpse of things to come.

Opposition to legalizing cannabis has historically centred around the gateway drug theory and its effect on mental health. But studies have debunked the purported link between cannabis use and a subsequent greater desire for stronger drugs.

A

A   Young cannabis plants
    inside a grow room at a
    mega-facility in Ontario,
    Canada, January 2021.
    Companies in the
    country have positioned
    themselves as global
    market leaders thanks
    to liberal policies.
B   Billboard adverts for
    cannabis in California,
    have raised fears
    that companies prey
    on young potential
    customers.

Fundamentally, what most likely encourages higher-risk drug consumption are environmental factors and the fact that drug dealers usually do not deal solely in one drug. It can also be in the interest of people with drug dependencies to initiate others and then supply them as a way of funding their own habits; with prohibition serving to create an explosive pyramid scheme. Nowhere is that more evident than with heroin, the use of which has exploded in the last half century.

More than 11 million people injected drugs in 2019 and, mainly due to needle-sharing, 1.4 million of those live with HIV and 5.6 million with hepatitis C. Heroin is the most dangerous drug of all – with about 20% of users becoming dependent – and its misuse remains a major public health issue, accounting for the majority of drug-related deaths in many countries. Heroin dependency is actually low risk and relatively non-problematic in a legal, managed setting but whole communities across the world have been negatively impacted by prohibition, which increases the risks associated with its use.

Gateway drug theory is a now-debunked idea that was previously mainstream, which posits that exposure to one drug naturally leads one towards desiring stronger substances.

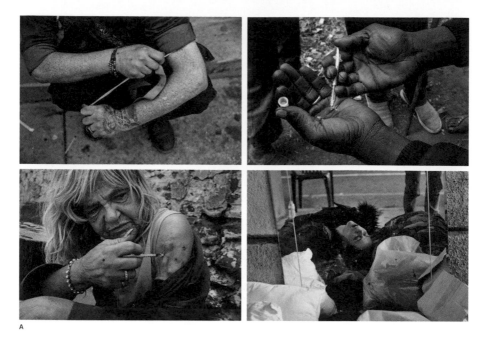

A

A   Individuals misusing heroin on the streets of San Francisco, California (top left), Nairobi, Kenya (top right), and Kensington, Philadelphia (bottom left and right). Often heroin becomes available in countries, such as Kenya, which was initially a passing stop on the trafficking route to Europe.

B   At the legendary New York club Studio 54 (shown here in c. 1979) cocaine was widely used and even provided to celebrity revellers by the venue's founders.

Dopamine is the reward chemical in the body that is released when certain internal pleasure centres are stimulated.

Those who do become dependent may exhibit the dreadful effects that street use can have as a result of struggling to find a vein to pierce, using water from a puddle to prepare the injection, turning to crime to support the habit or contracting a blood-borne disease. The drug produces feelings of euphoria and acts as a potent painkiller. It binds to the reward pathway, precipitating a flood of dopamine, essentially teaching the brain to take it and thus exerting strong control over behaviour. Prescribed heroin for those with dependencies leads to significant drops in drug-related crime and better health outcomes, as evidenced in Switzerland, and most recently in Middlesbrough in the UK.

People mostly use heroin to self-medicate trauma and if those issues remain unresolved then they are always likely to relapse. Overdoses can easily happen in environments used for illegal drug-taking, and they are often fatal. The gear might be unexpectedly potent, or people with low tolerances might be chasing the elusive feeling of their first dose.

Overdoses are relatively simple to reverse with naloxone, oxygen, CPR and by simply ensuring the person does not choke. In many places where people use drugs, trained first aiders are usually not on hand, but emergency workers in some countries are increasingly being equipped with the life-saving antidote naloxone, seeing people live for another day.

Conversely, the human body has the capacity to ingest substantial amounts of cocaine, redose after redose for days without sleeping, while often making people crave alcohol. When drinking and taking cocaine, the liver creates cocaethylene, which itself is psychoactive and addictive and is more toxic than either alcohol or cocaine alone. Long-term or excessive use of the drug can lead to overheating, strokes, disfigured noses, potentially lethal heart attacks and fatal overdoses, as well as an increased proneness to aggression, particularly when used with alcohol. Estimates that there are more than 20 million people using the drug worldwide – mainly in North America, Latin America and Europe – may well vastly underestimate its prevalence.

A

Though less suddenly than heroin, cocaine misuse kills thousands of people every year, but, much like alcohol, you will find people in bars in many major cities consuming it every night of the week. Next to cannabis and amphetamines, it is the third most popular illegal drug. People are reluctant to stop taking a drug that boosts their self-esteem, lubricates social situations and provides welcome relief from everyday stresses.

In a similar fashion for some, the offer of a drink underpins relationships with acquaintances, friends and lovers. Alcohol use is the cornerstone of many societies, and millions look forward all day to doing so in the evening. People often find each other's company far more interesting with a drink in hand, as it temporarily reduces stress. It makes you forget your sensibilities, senses and inhibitions, while compromising your judgment. Society caters to the often-excessive consumption of alcohol. Whole cities brace themselves for binge-drinking episodes, which have been normalized in popular culture thanks to light-hearted advertisements, widespread availability and sheer idiocy.

One in 20 deaths across the world are attributed to alcohol, and many more people will die from boozy accidents, fights and car crashes. Yet it is perversely considered a soft drug and ubiquitous in its availability, from 24-hour high-street shops and even petrol stations. It can have a destructive impact on internal organs and mental health, both swiftly and gradually, and studies have found that increased alcohol consumption rates are closely linked to rises in violent deaths. It is the only drug that induces dopamine and serotonin production, while blocking gaba (the chemical that helps make you think), yet it is ultimately a depressant.

Despite its dangerous effects, alcohol has been seen to be most detrimental to society when it is illegal.

Prohibitions in Iceland, Norway and the US in the early 20th century came amid speculation that 'men will walk upright now, women will smile and children will laugh'. In the US, prices swiftly tripled, quality control disappeared and police officers and judges were bribed as organized crime groups took over the roaring illegal alcohol trade. Deaths from contaminated alcohol rose – along with consumption rates – as beer became more difficult to come by but whisky was easy to find. Distilled spirits became more consumed than beers and wines, before returning to a sizeable minority after the repeal of prohibition in 1932.

Depressant drugs, including some that are referred to as 'downers', leave users feeling depressed, despite a possible euphoric period.

A   A woman collapses on a bench in the centre of Bristol, UK, after leaving a bar, October 2005.
B   Four men stand around a large copper kettle used to produce illegal liquor in the USA during prohibition, during which time deaths from contaminated alcohol skyrocketed.

B

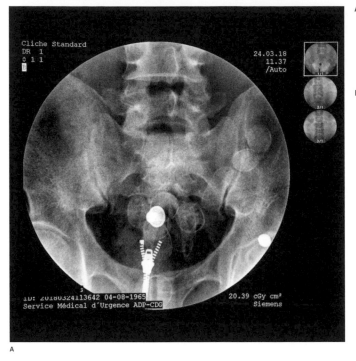

A

Mules is a pejorative word for people used to transport drugs across borders and within countries, possibly inside their bodies.

To avoid law-enforcement efforts, new drug-trafficking routes are constantly being carved out across the world, creating a trail of misery, destruction and inequality.

From the Latin American producer countries, cocaine bound for Europe often travels to Venezuela before it is shipped and flown to West Africa; otherwise it travels north to the US and Canada. More effective enforcement in Turkey has led to heroin being increasingly trafficked through East Africa, or going north from Afghanistan through Central Asia to Russia. In search of their final destination, drugs are ferried by impoverished, desperate people, often women, who may be referred to by the pejorative and stigmatizing term 'mules'. Meanwhile, pharmaceutical drugs are safely transported on ships and in planes.

In impoverished countries with weak institutions, the allure of easy money is even more likely to ensure a steady stream of pliable officials. Political parties are sponsored by drug cartels in some places and whole states have fallen under the direct influence of narco-traffickers, such as Guinea-Bissau, where the European street value of cocaine believed to pass through the country is about equal to its economic output. You cannot necessarily blame people for being tempted by a 'get rich quick' scheme. In Kenya the former governor of Nairobi, flamboyant Mike Sonko (b. 1975), and in Mombasa the current governor, Hassan Ali Joho (b. 1976), have been accused of drug-trafficking involvement – which they deny – while the main political party in Mozambique is believed to control heroin smuggling through the country. It is impossible to assess how far narco-corruption goes but the illegal drug economy is embedded into the legitimate economy through laundering operations.

The new transit countries, along with the producer states, are increasingly blighted by rising drug misuse and dependency thanks to growing availability. It is depressingly simple: if a drug suddenly arrives and you do not help people make informed choices, chaos ensues.

B

Almost nobody in Pakistan used heroin in 1979 but over 1 million did by 1985, amid surging production in neighbouring Afghanistan. Traditional drug smuggling channels through the Caribbean are more effectively policed than before, providing fresh opportunities for other Central American states, as well as displacing transit routes to fragile states in West Africa. Once enforcement reaches a critical threshold in any given region, the trade will inevitably shift again. The cycle continues.

Violence is not necessarily an inevitable part of the drug trade, since the majority of added value accrues during smuggling. Despite their faults, pharmaceutical corporations do not appear to involve themselves in conflict: deals are struck in boardrooms. But the lucrative, unregulated drug trade provides a mouthwatering bounty for organized crime groups to fight over. Around the world, drug money funds, and even creates, militant groups, which subsequently make political connections and may branch out into new rackets. In the Netherlands, traditionally relatively peaceful despite producing much of the world's synthetic drugs and being a central global transit hub, brutal murders are becoming more common and the country faces claims it is becoming a narco-state. Experts and police insiders are increasingly realizing that policing can leave disruptive power vacuums, causing increased violence.

A

United States v. Liborio S. Bellomo, et al.

B

A   Illegal drug production and transportation in Burma, Mexico and Mali have wreaked havoc and left many dead as efforts to crack down by the authorities have only brutalized the markets.

B   Poster board featuring photographs of indicted members of the Genovese organized crime family in New York City, USA, February 2006.

Drugs are moved across Europe thanks to cooperation between a number of organized crime groups, often with the involvement of Italian crime syndicate 'Ndrangheta, which has great influence over the cocaine trade and has contacts spanning most of the world. The profits the group has made in the drug trade have helped them become one of the continent's most powerful mafia, investing in various legitimate businesses, and their tentacles reach far and wide. In the UK, the most lucrative cocaine market in Europe, violent crime is rising steeply as rival gangs battle over the country's $7 billion drug market as falls in heroin and cocaine prices spark attempts at expansion to maintain profit levels.

For those locked out of the legitimate economy and marginalized, drug dealing can provide a glimmer of opportunity, while others are exploited from a young age. Refugees and migrants travelling to North America and Europe may follow similar paths to drugs, and are vulnerable to exploitation. This often fuels xenophobic public sentiment. At the higher end of organized crime groups, you are more likely to find a white Western European.

A

But how do drugs get past the authorities and into states in the first place?

They arrive in the US hidden in vehicles passing the border, by light aircraft and through passageways under the Mexican border. In 2020, Customs officials discovered a record-long narco-tunnel stretching more than 1,300 metres (4,256 ft) from Tijuana to San Diego, 21 metres (69 ft) underground. It had its own rail cart structure, elevator and drainage system. Half of Europe's cocaine arrives in Antwerp, Belgium. It is transported in tuna tins, hidden inside charcoal and pineapples, attached to the bottom of ships in magnetic boxes or alongside exotic fruit, with port officials paid off, and others following instructions in good faith. It may not even come on boats, but in submarines instead.

The case of aristocrat Jack Marrian (b. 1985) – who has been accused of smuggling £4.5 million of cocaine into Kenya by signing the import papers of a shipment – hints at how things are done. He denies the allegations. Antwerp's mayor Bart De Wever (b. 1970) has warned that corruption of officials and politicians is inevitable after the amount of cocaine seized rose to more than $1.7 billion in value.

Both the number of seizures of cocaine and the volumes confiscated in Europe are at all-time highs, underlining the failure of the war on drugs. Valedictory media reports occur when big hauls are made but an overwhelming majority pass unnoticed.

A maximum of 20% of the cocaine that enters the UK is seized but to have a serious long-term impact police would need to seize up to 80%. In Scotland, it is likely as little as 1% of heroin circulating is seized. Kilos of cocaine do not make it to their destination and, farcically, wash up on the shores of island nations, threatening ecosystems and biodiversity. The main danger of the illegal drug trade on the environment, however, is the corrupting influence of the profits made from it, which can leave governments impotent to reduce global warming because they do not control vast swathes of rural areas.

A   In March 2020, the US Border Patrol's San Diego Tunnel team seized more than 1.8 tonnes (2 tons) of drugs from part of the tunnel under the Otay Mesa area.
B   A seized narco-submarine on a Colombian Navy ship in March 2021. It contained several packages of cocaine destined for Mexico.
C   A Belgian police sniffer dog checks the back of a lorry at Antwerp port in September 2020.

A **narco-tunnel** is an underground passageway used to transport drugs without detection, most famously beneath the US-Mexico border.

Ecosystems describe multifaceted and interconnected systems of plants, animals and other organisms.

Biodiversity refers to the strength and diversity of an interdependent system of plants and animals.

Seizures of precursor drugs can be dangerous. In a tale emblematic of that for other drugs, the sale of tablets branded as ecstasy, but containing little or no MDMA and mixed with more toxic substitutes, surges after significant confiscations. This can be deadly, as can an absence of quality control, and the negligence and vindictiveness of some dealers.

Sales of N-ethylpentylone masquerading as ecstasy led to the hospitalization of 13 New Zealanders in 2018. The substance can cause psychosis. Other dealers add contaminants to both strengthen and stretch out their product. Six people in New York State died in 2021 after taking what was believed to be fentanyl-contaminated cocaine. There are countless more examples the world over.

A

Cryptocurrency is a digital form of decentralized currency, hosted across the Internet without central oversight or control.

The dark web is an encrypted part of the Internet not visible to conventional search engines and only accessible with specific software.

A   The rise of social media and encrypted messaging channels has created untold opportunities for drug sellers, and made law enforcement increasingly difficult as the trade becomes more incognito.
B   A screenshot of dark net marketplace Dream Market shows the wide variety of drugs available, including crystal meth, cocaine, hash and MDMA, accompanied by reviews from previous purchasers.
C   Users trying to access the original dark web drug marketplace, the Silk Road, are now confronted by this FBI notice; while founder Ross Ulbricht languishes in prison, serving life.

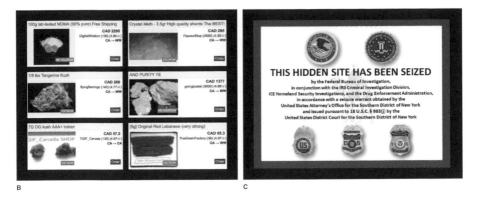

B   C

Organized crime groups are constantly professionalizing and adapting to market changes. Discount prices are offered from call centres, wares are advertised openly on social media and sellers compete to offer the fastest services. A survey of European young people suggested just one in five believed they would not be able to obtain heroin, cocaine, ecstasy or cannabis within a day.

The rise of cryptocurrency and the dark web in 2010 realigned the relationship between drug users and purveyors. Around 10% of drug-buyers now purchase via the dark net. There has not been a reported death from dark web drug competition. It has made it significantly easier for people to buy drugs more safely in bulk and to check sellers' feedback. Harm-reduction advice is often available too. The market largely floats above the chaos of street dealing. Any reduction in demand for street drugs, however, creates a smaller market with the same number of dealers, fuelling competition for territory.

A

Silk Road was the first, and most prominent, dark web marketplace in which drugs were sold. It was shut down by US officials but new versions were spawned.

Dependency is a chronic relapsing condition characterized chiefly by uncontrollable compulsive drug seeking and use.

Closures of dark net websites, like gang busts, do not have any lasting effect on the drug trade, as new marketplaces swiftly emerge. High-profile arrests, such as that of Silk Road founder Ross Ulbricht (b. 1984), make little lasting impact and, in any case, are rare. The dark web will always find ways to adapt and elude enforcement because it is both so popular – for vendors and customers – and difficult to decipher.

Evolving markets do not necessarily explain why more people are taking drugs than ever. People feel alienated and atomized in an era of less public investment, bullshit jobs, social media fixations, a growing mental health crisis and the pressures of consumerism and ingrained competition. In particular, people are increasingly taking psychedelics to obtain greater clarity and focus.

The stresses of the modern world explain why many city workers and mental health patients microdose psychedelics each day – to improve productivity and avert crises.

A Widespread prescriptions of amphetamine-based medications such as Ritalin and Adderall for hyperactive youngsters are increasingly being questioned in popular culture – as in this episode of *Family Guy*.

B These images show the areas of the brain contributing to visual processing while participants' eyes were closed. Researchers suggest these results indicate the complex visual hallucinations experienced when taking LSD.

While the vast majority of people will use drugs mostly non-problematically, dependency can create changes in the brain that interfere with the ability to resist intense urges. While the brain reduces the ability of cells in a person's reward circuit to respond to drug use, and the accompanying flood of dopamine – the happiness hormone – it is likely the key behavioural driver is attempts to deal with childhood trauma and social exclusion. A juncture can be reached where only drug use can bring relief, and pleasure. Eventually, negative consequences may begin to amass but the person will be unable or unwilling to give it up. One may experience similar desires for porn, new purchases, food, social media or even the news.

B

Areas of the brain used for visual processing, while participants' eyes were closed (2016)

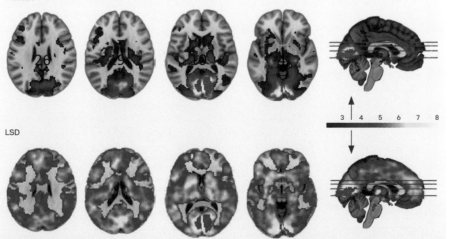

Placebo

LSD

3 4 5 6 7 8

EFFECTS ON INDIVIDUAL AND SOCIAL HEALTH

63

Dependency is still shrouded by moral mores and ideological fault lines over whether it represents a personal sin or failure for which one must face the consequences or a condition requiring treatment. An overwhelming body of research shows it is indeed the latter.

Methadone, the heroin replacement therapy, is often maligned but generally has positive public health benefits. Yet it constantly faces attacks from those who prefer to tout abstinence-based treatment. When facing the risk of being arrested, people with dependencies will largely refrain from seeking help, and if incarcerated, will often have little chance of receiving it.

Decriminalization has been shown around the world to be the best way to allow people to receive support.

A

B
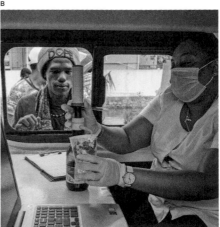

C

A   Posters on display near the dosage windows at a clinic in Maine, USA, January 2015. The clinic offers methadone (a synthetic opioid used to avoid withdrawal symptoms for people stopping heroin use and for chronic pain management) to patients as a part of their recovery process.

B   A man receives his methadone prescription in the Seychelles, November 2019. The rise of new trafficking routes through East Africa has led to a heroin boom in the Seychelles over the past decade.

C   In shopping malls across the world, people spend their incomes on a constantly evolving array of consumer goods that mark out status and class. The satisfaction that each purchase brings is often short-lived.

Conveniently, most governments are broadly unconcerned, neoliberal economies run on trauma (the true gateway drug) and feed off fear, as addiction expert Gabor Maté has argued in the podcast *Under the Skin*. People's basic psychological needs are often unmet owing to the nature of society and the economy. Consumerism relies on the idea that people are insufficient without an external fix, thus intrinsically encouraging addictive mentalities and non-rational behaviour. The economic order exists on the premise that people will continue to buy ever-increasing amounts of stuff. Yet society creates artificial needs – through advertisements, peer pressure and the very make-up of the physical world and parts of the Internet – rather than helping provide what people truly crave: happiness, health, stability and connection with nature.

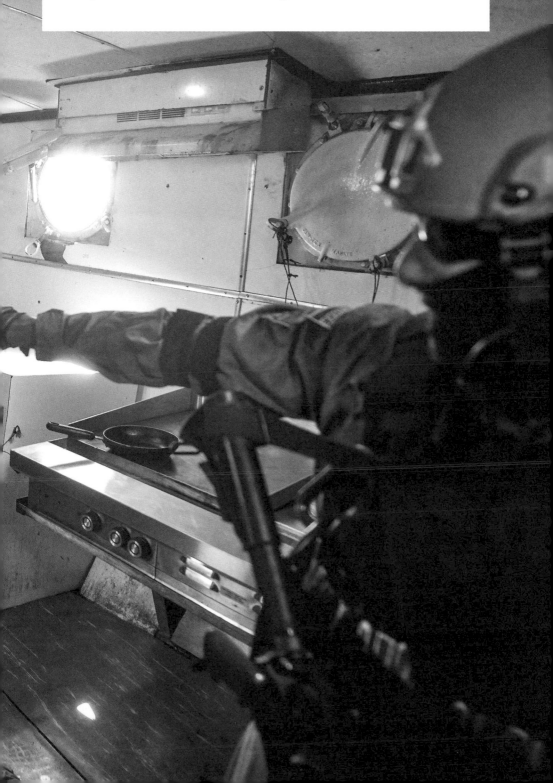

A   Poster caricaturing Nixon and
     featuring a swastika in place
     of an 'x', designed and printed
     by students at the Rhode
     Island School of Design in 1968
     when Nixon was campaigning
     for the presidency, claiming he
     would bring 'peace with
     honour' in the Vietnam War.
B/C In the 1960s people in the West
     began experimenting with a
     new cache of drugs, including
     heroin and opium, and drug
     use increasingly became
     associated with various
     countercultures that presented
     radically different worldviews
     to mainstream cultures.

A

Wars usually break out between states, tribes or mercenary forces fighting on behalf of political interests. But in June 1971, then US president Richard Nixon (1913–94) declared that the scale of drug use in the country represented a national emergency and called for a 'war on drugs'. But how can you defeat drugs? Was eradicating the demand for them ever a realistic policy objective?

Drugs were seen throughout the 1960s as a potent counter-cultural symbol of rebellion and political dissent as use of cannabis, LSD, cocaine, amphetamines and heroin rose. It became the third most important issue for voters in the US amid hyperbolic media reports and grandstanding politicians sowing fear. 'It's not that psychedelics are dangerous, it's that they give you dangerous ideas,' ethnopharmacologist Dennis McKenna (b. 1950) says.

Thus, amid unfolding disaster in Vietnam, the wily Republican Nixon moved to cast drugs as 'public enemy number one' and dramatically increased funding, including on treatment, to eradicate the supply and use of drugs. This was a war he said he could win, despite the fact that the policy was predicated on an ignorance of drugs and a misplaced faith in the power of the law to regulate human vice, as author Tom Feiling comments in *The Candy Machine: How Cocaine Took Over the World* (2009).

B   C

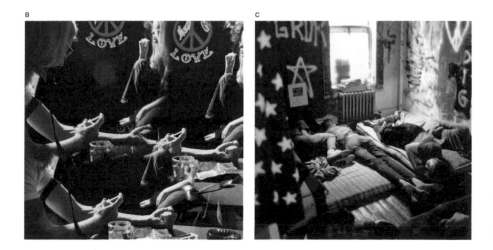

The conflict sought to strangle the supply of drugs, press other countries for action, and de-glamourize drugs and reduce demand at home.

A First Lady Nancy
Reagan accepts a
cheque for $150,000
from multinational
company Proctor
& Gamble in 1987
on behalf of her
crusading anti-drugs
organization, 'Just
Say No' club.
B US President Bill
Clinton signs a law
enforcement-focused
bill attempting
to curtail use of
methamphetamine
in 1996. The bill largely
failed amid the rise
of small labs and
growing demand.
C Person brought to jail
under the influence
of drugs or alcohol and
placed in isolation in a
cell until they sober up
– without the provision
of harm-reduction
measures.

Across the US, measures including harsh mandatory minimum sentences and no-knock warrants were also pushed through to intimidate drug dealers, while other countries were strongly encouraged to adopt the same 'tough on drugs' enforcement approaches. Millions of non-violent offenders were arrested for using drugs. As mass incarceration began in the 1980s, and was supercharged in the following decade thanks to Bill Clinton's (b. 1946) 'three strikes for life' policy, a domino effect was set off around the world after prohibitionist international treaties driven by the US had laid the groundwork for the war on drugs. The treaties also stressed the need for United Nations member states to offer treatments for dependency in hospital, but drugs were later described by the United Nations' economic and social council as 'a powerful instrument of the most hideous crime against mankind'.

A

B

No-knock warrants
are permissions
issued to police,
often on suspicion
of drug offences,
to enter and search
premises without
any warning.

The **United Nations** is
the US-headquartered
global institution
whose members
and security council
act to set common
standards and rules,
including drug policy.

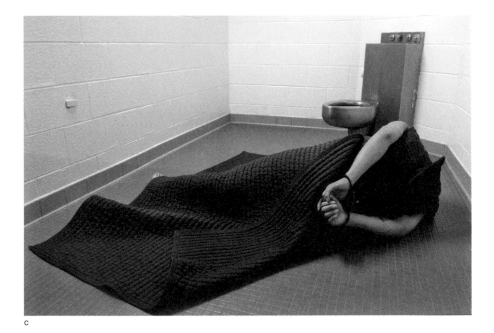

c

Nixon may have explicitly sought a tool to wage a crusade against certain segments of society. His domestic policy chief John Ehrlichman (1925–99) confessed: 'The Nixon campaign in 1968 and the Nixon White House after that had two enemies: the anti-war left and Black people... We knew we couldn't make it illegal to be either against the war or Blacks, but by getting the public to associate the hippies with marijuana and Blacks with heroin, and then criminalizing both heavily, we could disrupt those communities. We could arrest their leaders, raid their homes, break up their meetings and vilify them night after night after night on the evening news. Did we know we were lying about the drugs? Of course we did.'

Controls around the world have been rooted in racial prejudice and other forms of social control. Many of the initial prohibitions were at least partly fuelled by bigotry underpinned by fears of foreigners and minority groups, and perceived threats to labour markets. The notion that drugs used by people of colour were deviant was a prevailing undercurrent.

A

Conversations about drug use were always racialized: opium was Chinese (though Europeans had long sold and used it), African Americans snorted cocaine and Mexicans smoked 'marijuana'. The Opium Exclusion Act, passed in 1909, criminalized the smoking of the drug but did not prohibit its use as a drink as part of an alcohol tincture, which was more popular with non-Chinese people. Officials raised fears over African Americans raping women under the influence of cocaine and Mexicans harming upper-class white women after smoking cannabis.

People of colour and the poor have continued to bear the brunt of the war on drugs. Marginalized communities have been most affected by drug-related crime and harm from the tandem collateral damage of militarized policing.

B

Despite implicit racial and socioeconomic biases within the war on drugs, it was framed as a humanitarian mission against 'an age-old evil' in the 1961 UN treaty. As in most wars, evidence was increasingly ignored and politicians favoured law and order in principle over public health in practice. Governments, authoritarian in nature, could only seem to ratchet up the draconian measures, possibly unable to act in any other way in areas deemed to be related to crime.

Ironically, attempts at a global crackdown came just as world markets began to open up like never before. The globalization of drugs thrust what was previously kept within individual subcultures into the mainstream. Suddenly, one could easily smoke cannabis in an English village, shoot heroin in an Iranian city or sniff cocaine on a remote island. Profits for organized crime groups across the world spiralled upwards. Had the production and sale of such drugs been legal, legitimate businesses would have capitalized on the trade. As the drugs were illegal, criminal entrepreneurs filled the gap.

Where does this money go? Back into treatment or community services as it could do under a legally regulated model? No, it is often laundered through the legitimate economy – creating hollow businesses – or spent on weapons or invested in other forms of criminality. More than half of the illegal market profits, valued in hundreds of billions a year, is believed to be laundered through the legitimate economy, but less than 1% is seized.

The US spends around $50 billion on the war on drugs each year, with a tiny fraction of the estimated $1 trillion in the last half century invested in public health measures to reduce harms. The war has also now been outsourced to client regimes in Latin America, who become indebted to the US from the purchase of their weapons and military hardware. Washington's foreign policy focus in the region from the late 1980s shifted from containing communism to opening markets and the stemming of illegal drug flows. It also claimed to be strengthening democracy, despite countless progressive movements and democratic governments being undermined and overthrown with CIA backing. Described by scholars as 'narco-colonialism' and 'drug war capitalism', the drug war has been identified as a major driver of investment for the burgeoning security industry. It has financed right-wing paramilitaries who have waged a dual war against traffickers and dissidents while often taking control of drug supply themselves.

A

A Mexican journalists take part in a protest against the murder of, and lack of justice for, their colleague Javier Valdez Cárdenas, an expert on the country's drug cartels, who was killed in 2017.
B An agent on patrol at the US-Mexican border rounds up a substantial cache of cannabis in January 2009.
C Bodies of two men killed druing a shooting in Culiacán, Sinaloa, Mexico, July 2019. Residents claim that despite the life sentence received by drug lord Joaquín Guzmán neither the rate of violence nor drug trafficking will diminish.

Ultra-violent drug gangs throughout Latin America emerged in an attempt to control the drug trade, and many have expanded into illegal logging, people-smuggling and seemingly legitimate businesses while remaining intertwined with local politicians, police and civil militias. After the escalation of the war on drugs in Mexico upon the orders of then-president Felipe Calderón (b. 1962) in 2006, drug violence escalated dramatically amid the presence of tens of thousands of soldiers and police in the streets and the countryside.

The drug war turned Mexico into the world's deadliest conflict zone outside of Syria: more than 170,000 people have been murdered in drug-related violence since the conflict was intensified in 2006 and over 37,000 have disappeared and remain unaccounted for, not least the 43 students whose murders in 2014 appeared to be covered up by corrupt officials, sparking outrage. All across the country, families are searching for their lost sons and daughters. Drug gangs have brazenly taken over whole towns and the instability has had a profound effect on the country's economy.

It is impossible to overstate the scale of violence, depravity and wreckage it has caused. Mexico has been torn apart. Attempts to capture drug lords turn towns into war zones and demonstrate how the army can be outgunned by better-resourced private armies, while a culture of impunity reigns even for many of those apprehended.

According to former deputy British prime minister Nick Clegg (b. 1967), Calderón acknowledged privately that the drug war was unwinnable: 'He had made his whole name in Mexican politics as "I'm going to win the war on drugs". He said to me, "Do you think there will ever be the regulated sale of drugs in Britain or America? Because I've come to the view" – and I remember he said it with such pathos – "that we've spent years trying to wage this war on drugs that is unwinnable. You will never win unless you can squeeze out criminality by moving towards the regulation of drugs."'

This is because the rising demand for cocaine, cannabis and other drugs around the world spawned a new class of organized crime actors in the region who pose serious challenges to state power, thanks to their billions and heavily armed private armies.

A

A Escobar's Medellín cartel used the airstrip at Norman's Cay, Bahamas, to transport cocaine to the US. Escobar and one of his key collaborators, Camillo Zapata Vasquez, amassed a huge fortune from the drug trade and lived in luxury during the 1980s. Shown here are (top right) Escobar's luxury apartment 'Monaco' in Medllín, Colombia, and 'Le Marroquin' in Bogotá, Colombia – a sumptuous replica castle with secret passageways – owned by Vasquez.

B Posters of the deceased Escobar proclaiming 'Pablo for President–Sovereignty-Independence' were ordered to be removed by authorities in Bogotá, Colombia, in 2006.

Colombia's Pablo Escobar (1949 – 93), the so-called 'King of Cocaine', effectively monopolized the cocaine trade into the US in the 1980s under the control of his Medellín cartel. Systematically buying off politicians and police, Escobar – the seventh-richest man in the world at one stage, possessing $76 billion – developed a Robin Hood reputation by giving to poor people neglected by the government and the market.

Colombia reached a state of unprecedented crisis thanks to conflicts between the government and the cartels (and simply between the cartels), often fuelled and escalated by Escobar, who funded a group of guerrillas who stormed the Supreme Court and killed half the country's top judges. He was himself killed in 1993 after an extended game of cat and mouse with Colombian authorities and DEA (Drug Enforcement Administration) agents. Meanwhile, ever greater opportunities for drug trafficking emerged in Mexico for those who had started out as the middlemen for Colombian narcos trafficking cocaine into the US.

A

Joaquín Guzmán (b. 1957), also known as El Chapo, oversaw the expansion of the Mexican Sinaloa cartel as it became the most powerful organized crime group in the country, traversing the entire southern US border. Institutions and officials had long been corrupted, but there was relative peace until the declaration of Calderón's war in 2006 – though he claimed inter-cartel violence was inevitable.

There are long-standing allegations that Guzman's cartel was in effect allied with the DEA and supplied US authorities with information on rival groups, helping them on their road to hegemony. DEA leaks are also reported to have led to brutal massacres, with the head of its 'Sensitive Information Unit' in Mexico on trial in 2020 for selling secrets. Mexican politicians and law-enforcement figures, including former secretary of public security Genaro García Luna (b. 1968), have also been accused of assisting drug traffickers, not least the Sinaloa cartel. But justice has been uneven. An analysis of crime figures by NPR found that only one in ten of people arrested, prosecuted or sentenced for drug, organized crime and weapons offences had ties to the Sinaloa cartel up until 2010. Drug laws – and attempts to enforce them – create more harm than the drugs themselves. Money corrupts: that is the 'age-old evil', not drugs *per se*.

During the 1980s, the CIA funded the Contras, a right-wing rebel group in Nicaragua connected to cocaine trafficking, to overthrow the elected socialist Sandinista government. A Senate inquiry chaired by future presidential candidate John Kerry (b. 1943) warned: 'In the name of supporting the Contras, [officials] abandoned the responsibility our government has for protecting our citizens from all threats to their security and well-being.' The CIA later conceded it had failed to 'cut off relationships with individuals supporting the Contra programme who were alleged to have engaged in drug trafficking'.

This came after the so-called 'cocaine coup' in 1980, which saw Bolivia's left-wing interim president Lidia Gueiler Tejada (1921–2011) replaced by a right-wing junta backed by traffickers, following a CIA-backed coup. Mass murder, extrajudicial killings and the systematic use of torture ensued.

In the next decade, in Venezuela, an anti-drugs unit funded by the CIA was found to have smuggled more than 900 kg (1,984 lb) of cocaine into the US with the knowledge of agency officials. Former DEA chief Robert Bonner (b. 1942) said at the time there was 'at least some participation in approving or condoning' the drug smuggling by the CIA.

A   Ahead of his extradition to the US, El Chapo, the world's most-wanted drug trafficker, is shown being escorted by security forces at a navy hangar in Mexico City in 2016, after being recaptured by Mexican authorities six months after he escaped from a maximum-security prison through an elaborate tunnel.

B   US President Ronald Reagan holds up a badge proclaiming 'If you like Cuba, you'll love Nicaragua' as he speaks in the White House in 1986 to Nicaraguan Contra supporters. The right-wing counter-revolutionaries were funded by the US despite being implicated in cocaine trafficking and human rights abuses.

C   Contra rebels – who often targeted civilians – patrolling the northern mountains of Nicaragua in 1987. The rebels eventually achieved the goal of regime change sought by the US, who did not want governments in the region to redistribute wealth and land.

Around this time, the US also established a certification process to ensure foreign governments were cooperating with the war on drugs. The process was linked with aid – which declined in real terms as drug war funding rose. Both Mexico and Colombia have received billions in aid that has regularly gone towards bolstering their armies, often with US-made equipment, despite their poor human rights records.

In Bolivia, in 2006, the later exiled former president Evo Morales (b. 1959) – who made his name politically as leader of a coca growers' union – legalized cultivation and banned fumigation before expelling the DEA officers who had given one-off payments to farmers for each field of coca destroyed, without providing viable alternatives.

A

Crop substitution is replacing on a sustainable basis the growing of lucrative crops such as coca and opium with non-psychoactive plants.

The **1961 Single Convention on Narcotic Drugs** is one of the most significant, sweeping UN treaties, transposed largely from US law, prohibiting drugs.

A   Pictured in 1955, indigenous Bolivian women pick coca leaves in the mountains near Chulumani, Bolivia, during the harvest.
B   In December 2000 Bolivian coca farmers throw leaves into the air as part of a protest to show that they will not cease cultivation of coca despite government claims to have eradicated it.
C   Bags of coca leaves confiscated from farmers in Bolivia in May 2008, on the assumption that they are intended for the production of cocaine.

Morales argued that increased demand for cocaine in the US should not rob indigenous people of ancient traditions, as well as coca's benefits. He called on the UN to remove it from its list of prohibited drugs. 'This leaf represents... the hope of our people,' Morales told the UN General Assembly in 2007, holding a coca leaf aloft. He negotiated crop substitution plans while supporting the farmers, leading to a 12% decrease in the area used to grow coca in 2011, and engendering a greater sense of security for farmers.

The US Department of State said Bolivia, which was implementing socialist reforms under its first ever indigenous president, had 'failed demonstrably to meet its obligations under international counternarcotic agreements'. The US withheld approval for Bolivia's anti-drugs policies (dictating whether they received aid or trade benefits), even though it certified close allies Colombia and Peru, which both saw coca cultivation rise. Eventually, Bolivia unilaterally withdrew from the 1961 Single Convention on Narcotic Drugs, amid objections from Western states, before re-acceding in 2013 with an allowance for the chewing of the coca leaf.

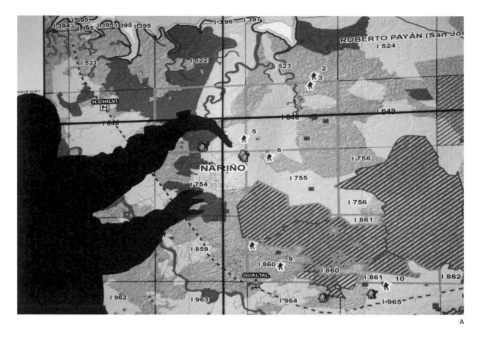

A

Motivated by ideological concerns, the drug war is fought with no consideration of the future. It is almost as though it is a war intended to continue in perpetuity. Eradication efforts often do little to address the root causes of why poor farmers produce crops for drugs. These include non-payment for crops through legitimate channels and the lack of development of alternative industries.

Morales tweeted in 2021 of US authorities: 'The so-called "war on drugs" is an excuse to attack progressive and anti-imperialist governments. It is a cover for your geopolitical interests.' Of Colombia's $1.3 billion initial aid package from the US, a mere fraction was allocated to crop switching – compared to about half in military aid. If you burn a few fields, others will swiftly pop up before the original ones gradually heal. With the price of cocaine vastly inflated due to prohibition, it seems only legal regulation can make growing other crops attractive for many farmers who do so willingly.

B

Agent Orange is a defoliant chemical infamously dropped by US forces on Vietnamese villages, leaving people with life-changing injuries and hereditary illnesses.

Carcinogenic describes a substance capable of causing cancer in humans and other animals.

A   A police officer shows a map highlighting coca-growing areas in Tumaco, Colombia, in February 2020 after the country's defence minister said the military would step up an offensive against drug-trafficking gangs responsible for clearing thousands of hectares of protected national parks for coca plantations.

B   In June 2008 a plane sprays coca plants in El Catatumbo, Colombia, with fumigation chemicals to prevent the crop from being grown. About 3,000 hectares (7,500 acres) were fumigated in the area.

Police in Colombia have killed coca farmers protesting against impending forced eradication after they were threatened by traffickers to take part in the demonstrations. Activists who criticize the government for not doing more to offer alternatives to coca production have to go into hiding. The growers, often indigenous people, have been caught in the crossfire and killed during raids on smugglers. Meanwhile, helicopters and planes fumigate coca fields from the air with toxic chemicals that have been compared to Agent Orange to destroy crops in the second most biodiverse country in the world. Livelihoods and people's health are seriously harmed, reportedly causing cancers and birth defects, yet the crops are simply replanted in the same spaces as the spraying method is ineffective in the long term. The only solution is to thoroughly salt the earth, which would prevent anything from growing. Aerial fumigations were eventually suspended after it emerged that the chemicals used were likely carcinogenic. Destructive new US-supported aerial spraying tactics have resumed, and aggressive state anti-drugs strategies have been blamed for fuelling fresh cycles of violence. Imagine if the government simply regulated the growing of coca. Utopian thinking, but it seems likely it would instil greater order.

In 2019, two-thirds of the 1,633 tonnes (1,800 tons) of cocaine produced globally (an estimated record) hailed from Colombia. The steep and unprecedented rise in the amount of land cultivated for coca there occurred after the guerrilla group the Farc disbanded and competition between buyers as the market splintered pushed up prices for coca.

Drug trafficking through Central America – through which almost all of the cocaine intended for the US passes – has carved out deep routes of destruction.

In El Salvador, the murder rate has reached higher levels than during its civil war, as rival cartels battle for control of the lucrative supply lines. In Guatemala the murder rate has doubled since 1999, with the money generated by the cocaine trade suspected of equalling that of the legitimate economy. It is a similar story in the Bahamas, the Dominican Republic and Nicaragua. States such as Honduras have been criticized for enthusiastically fighting a war on drugs in partnership with the US in order to bolster their own fragile grip on power.

A

A   A Venezuelan migrant in Colombia working as a collector of coca leaves shows his bloodied, battered hands as he works at a plantation in February 2019.
B   The corpse of a man with a notice attributing his murder to a drug cartel lies in the port city of Acapulco, Mexico, in 2011. The area was once popular with international tourists and celebrities, but large swathes have since become no-go zones as cartels fight for territory to sell drugs and extort businesses.

The Farc were founded in 1964 as the armed wing of the Communist Party in Colombia. It was partly funded by the drug trade.

B

Former US agents have claimed cartel leaders embraced the war on drugs as it increased prices and eliminated small time dealers. A top Bolivian cartel chief, Jorge Roman, said it was actually 'good for business', according to former undercover officer Michael Levine, author of *The Big White Lie* (1993). 'Where crime and corruption reign and drug money perverts the economy, the state no longer has a monopoly on the use of force and citizens no longer trust their leaders and public institutions,' said Antonio Maria Costa (b. 1941), United Nations Office on Drugs and Crime (UNODC) executive director, in 2008. 'As a result, the social contract is in tatters and people take the law into their own hands.'

What the dealers fear are effective demand reduction initiatives, but business is booming and the amount spent on policing drug use and the trade has long dwarfed the amount spent on treatment, a more effective form of reducing demand for drugs. A twentieth of US anti-drugs money has been spent on treatment in some years this century. It is estimated that investment in domestic US enforcement is three times more effective in reducing consumption than a similar investment in decreasing production in the source country.

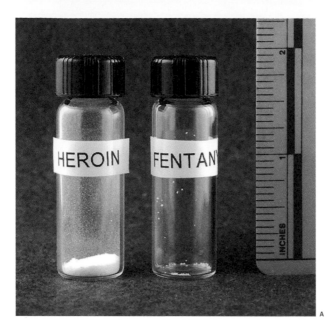

A   On the left, a lethal dose of heroin; on the right, a lethal dose of fentanyl, the powerful synthetic opioid that is similar to morphine but is 50 to 100 times more potent and available on prescription.
B   Afghan workers scrape the opium sap from poppy bulbs in May 2005. Afghanistan remains the largest producer of the heroin base ingredient in the world. Many farmers are dependent on money from these crops to feed their families.
C   A man smoking heroin in Kabul in 2005. Afghanistan became a narco-state after Soviet and US invasions led the Taliban to turn to narcotics as a source of income. This led many in the country to become dependent as availability swiftly grew.

Meanwhile, changing drug demand in the US after the partial legalization of cannabis and surging opioid use, along with tighter border security, has led traffickers to diversify into more potent and concentrated drugs, such as fentanyl. Efforts to address why people take drugs are scant.

On the other side of the world, attempts by the US to eradicate the production of heroin have been similarly flawed and sparked accusations it helped move supply of the drug westwards.

Afghanistan produces the vast majority of the world's illegal opium. Production soared from less than 100 tonnes (98 tons) a year in the 1970s to 2,000 tonnes (1,968 tons) by 1991 to fund the war effort against the invading Soviets in 1979, which was also financed to the tune of $3 billion in arms by the US. The opium crop plummeted to 185 tonnes (182 tons) in 2000 as the Taliban imposed a ban on cultivation to win international support. But after the declaration of the war on terror and the American invasion in 2001, production accelerated once more – from 3,000 tonnes (2,953 tons) in the next year to more than 9,000 tonnes (8,858 tons) by 2017.

US forces were in Afghanistan for two decades, a period of unprecedented growth in opium cultivation and heroin production that a Senate report admitted saw the military 'ignore the drug trade flourishing in front of its eyes'. The country has been described as the world's first true narco-state: where drugs 'dominate the economy, define political choices and determine the fate of foreign interventions'. The brother of the former president Hamid Karzai (b. 1957), a suspected player in the opium trade, received regular payments from the CIA throughout the 2000s. It came after American intelligence officers are claimed to have effectively consented to opium exports throughout the 1990s. 'Everyone chose to ignore it,' according to Afghanistan expert Ahmed Rashid. Decades later, in 2013, plans to go after Taliban commanders and drug lords were abandoned due to concerns it would destabilize Afghanistan and undermine potential peace talks, before the US' ignominious exit from the country.

B

C

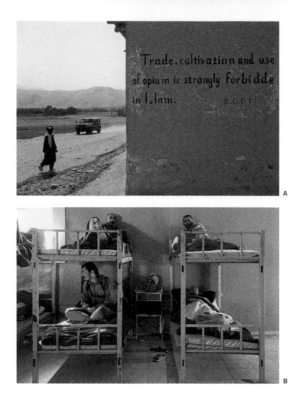

A

B

Iron Tempest was a US operation launched in late 2017 in a failed attempt to destroy drug labs in Afghanistan.

A   An anti-drugs message written in 2001 on the side of a building in the Afghan opposition capital of Faizabad. Although the opposition has, like the Taliban, opposed opium production, they have not had the means to enforce the ban on poppy farming.
B   People dependent on drugs in a hospital for drug treatment in Kabul in October 2021. They were rounded up by the Taliban soon after they took control.
C   Poster satirizing the activities of HSBC – the most notorious multinational bank to have been publicly found to have profited from international criminal schemes.

Evidently, the US has had innumerable opportunities to substantially dent the global supply of drugs but it has not seized them. Realpolitik, dogma and ideology have stood in the way, proving this is a conflict of management and control, rather than one in which victory is truly sought. Plus, again, we see attempts to control and disrupt the drug trade do more harm than the intoxicants themselves.

Researchers have found that many of the labs in northern Helmand bombed by US fighter jets from 2016–17 were just farmhouses or had been inactive for months. The costs of the campaign and the destruction it caused did far more harm than good, and the Iron Tempest operation is now over. The Taliban, back in charge, have pledged to end opium growing but there is serious scepticism over whether that is possible due to the financial rewards.

Poppy production is growing and expanding to ever more countries, with the trade inevitably corrupting local economies. Between 2009 and 2018, UNODC data shows that opium poppy cultivation across 50 countries more than doubled. Even if the US had taken down Afghan production, Pakistan, Burma or Mexico – which also produce significant amounts of opium and heroin – would be primed to step into the gap, or domestic production could increase.

But where does all this money go?

A 2012 US court ruling found the British bank HSBC allowed at least $881 million of Sinaloa cartel drug trafficking money to be laundered through its accounts. Prosecutors said Mexican authorities had warned HSBC in 2008 that it was referred to by a drug lord as 'the place to launder money'. The bank was fined a record $1.9 billion, about a month's income for HSBC's American subsidiary. Its chief executive, Stephen Green (b. 1948), joined the UK government as a trade minister, and Paul Thurston (b. 1953), who was in charge of HSBC Mexico, was promoted. A *New York Times* editorial reported: 'Federal and state authorities have chosen not to indict HSBC...on charges of vast and prolonged money laundering, for fear that criminal prosecution would topple the bank and...endanger the financial system.'

c

They call it crime.
We call it business.

For a bank that was founded to finance the illegal opium trade, we've certainly stayed true to our roots.

We laundered hundreds of millions of pounds for the world's largest and most violent drug cartels, moved money across borders for everyone from Al-Qaeda to ISIS, and helped countries like Iran, Sudan and North Korea bypass UN sanctions.

Whether you need help evading taxes, laundering your drug profits, selling weapons to brutal dictators, or funding investment in the fossil fuels that will exterminate life on Earth, give us a call.

HSBC
The world's criminal bank

A

Known drug launderer Banamex (Mexico's second-largest bank) was purchased by Citibank (founded as the city bank of New York) in 2001, which then shared in the profits as it continued to launder drug money – only receiving slaps on the wrists from authorities when instances came to light. Mossack Fonseca, the law firm at the centre of the Panama Papers revelations, was found to have represented former head of the Guadalajara cartel Caro Quintero's (b. 1952) offshore company and effectively refused to cooperate with authorities seeking to obtain one of his properties. Seemingly there will always be another bank, or another state, willing to act on the behalf of traffickers, so long as they have enough cash.

Disproportionately, the true punishments are meted out to the most vulnerable and the death penalty imposed even for minor cases. States claim to protect their populations from drugs by instilling terror. In Iran, China, Indonesia, Saudi Arabia, Malaysia, Singapore and across a number of other countries, tens of thousands of people have been officially executed by the state for drug offences since the millennium. These people are often from the lowest level of the trade and may have had no other economic choice or were coerced into it.

It is common for them not to have legal aid and be subjected to sham trials. In Saudi Arabia, hundreds of people accused of non-violent, drug-related offences have been executed in the past decade. A number of people on death row were prominent critics of the regime and arrested on the pretext of drug offences believed to have been false.

Across the world, thousands of people – many of whom are illiterate and from impoverished backgrounds – are estimated to be awaiting execution after being forced to act as drug traffickers and sellers. Due to rampant inequality and starvation, there is always a steady stream of people who are either prepared to take such roles or forced to ply drugs under duress. This, of course, fails to truly impact the drug trade or ensnare key players who can afford expensive legal defences.

A   Activists in Berlin, Germany, throw fake money into the air while demanding greater transparency in new legislation following the ongoing Panama Papers scandal, 2016.
B   Three Iranian drug dealers hang from nooses as it snows in a square in Qom, Iran, in 2008. Ten other criminals were also executed on the same day.
C   Protesters in Makati City, Philippines, light candles and demonstrate against the planned state execution of a mother-of-two in Indonesia for smuggling heroin, April 2015.

The **Panama Papers** scandal was a series of leaked papers from disgraced offshore law firm Mossack Fonseca, revealing how the world's rich and powerful avoid paying taxes.

In the Philippines, the state wages war against low-level offenders and traffickers. These people are public enemy number one and extrajudicial killing squads, often made up of vigilantes, have executed more than 27,000 people, including many children, since June 2016. More than 140,000 people are in prison ahead of trial on dubious drug charges, according to activists, after far-right president Rodrigo Duterte (b. 1945) effectively declared war against 'illegal drug personalities' and claimed the Philippines had become a narco-state. He offered bounties to the police for killing those suspected of using drugs or being dealers, and even urged members of the public to do the same. The Philippines has continued to receive substantial financial support, chiefly from the US, even though the war on drugs and the declaration of martial law have been used as a pretext to attack land defenders opposing logging and mining and has created a culture of impunity and fear. In 2021, the International Criminal Court belatedly sanctioned a full investigation into his war on drugs.

There are countless stories of well-connected people getting off scot-free in the Philippines. Duterte's main critic, Senator Leila de Lima (b. 1959), has been detained since February 2017 on what Human Rights Watch has described as politically motivated drug charges in apparent retaliation for leading a Senate inquiry into the killings. Meanwhile, the chief of police, who was accused of receiving profits from the sale of confiscated methamphetamine by protected officers, was only initially made to stand down.

A

A The corpse of a suspected drug seller found under a bridge in Manila, Philippines, July 2016. He was one of thousands of victims of a state-backed, vigilante-style executions in the Philippines. After President Rodrigo Duterte was swept to power in June 2016, he pledged to kill people who use and sell drugs in an all-out war.

B This 2014 graph shows how almost half of the US' gigantic prison population was incarcerated for drug offences. This has driven a rapid growth of the total US jail population to now number more than 2 million.

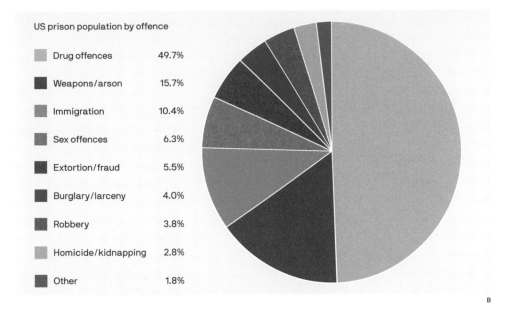

US prison population by offence

	Offence	%
	Drug offences	49.7%
	Weapons/arson	15.7%
	Immigration	10.4%
	Sex offences	6.3%
	Extortion/fraud	5.5%
	Burglary/larceny	4.0%
	Robbery	3.8%
	Homicide/kidnapping	2.8%
	Other	1.8%

B

At the same time, prisons remain full of non-violent people who use drugs and offenders who have only committed minor possession and growing offences. More than one in five inmates in jails across 30 major countries have a drug offence as their main charge, with that figure rising to half in the US and over four-fifths in federal Thai prisons. The proportion of those who use drugs themselves, and had committed crimes to fund their dependency, likely rises even higher. Rather than being rehabilitated, the prisoners are often left to become hardened criminals as they try to keep their heads above water in drug-filled prisons where there is far more violence than outside.

A

A penal approach seems to make more people dependent on drugs. The think tank Reform found that one in seven prisoners in the UK become dependent inside, and a quarter of US prisoners are dependent on opioids according to the Pew Trust. Many serve short sentences, and due to an absence of rehabilitation and effective solitary confinement for long periods, their issues only become worse.

Socioeconomic inequalities, economic exclusion, violence and exploitation often force young people from ethnic minorities to ply the trade. Drug laws provide the police carte blanche to search innocent citizens for merely an alleged whiff of cannabis. In the US, the draconian application of drug laws drives racial disparities and mass incarceration. Although Black and white people consume cannabis and other drugs at the same rate, the former are up to four times more likely to be arrested for possession, and make up 60% of the prison population.

In the UK, a fifth of those prosecuted under cannabis laws are Black, despite making up 1 in 25 of the population. In the US, nearly half are Black or Latino, despite those ethnic groups accounting for less than a third of the population.

Imprisonment for drug offences has resulted in exponential rises in prison populations around the world at a time when some countries are increasingly privatizing their jails. Thailand's penal population surged to the sixth highest volume globally after former prime minister Thaksin Shinawatra (b. 1974) launched a crackdown in 2003. More than 2,800 were killed extrajudicially by police, and Thailand now has two-fifths of Southeast Asia's prison population, despite having only a tenth of its total population.

A   Two inmates, likely ill from opiate detox, are monitored in the medical care section of a US jail in 2015. In recent years increasing numbers of opiate- and heroin-addicted inmates have been sent to serve time in places that only offer abstinence-based treatment.

B   Female inmates at a women's prison in Bangkok, Thailand, sit with their children for their one-hour-a-week visit in 2002. More than 80% of prisoners were serving sentences on drug-related charges.

C   Hundreds of inmates in Bangkok's overcrowded Klong Prem prison during a roll call in August 2000. Thailand's Department of Corrections claimed there were over 200,000 prisoners in its 133 prisons nationwide, double the number of just three years prior: a consequence of laws allowing street-level drug users to be jailed.

Noam Chomsky is a left-wing US intellectual and the 'father of modern linguistics'. He is highly critical of the USA's position in the modern world.

The futility of the murderous policies was eventually acknowledged by the government. 'The world has lost the war on drugs, not only Thailand,' justice minister Paiboon Koomchaya (b. 1955) told Reuters in 2016. 'We have clear numbers that drug use has increased over the past three years', despite suppression efforts, he added. Fast forward five years, and the country's parliament passed a law emphasizing prevention and treatment over punishment, anxious to ease pressure on an overcrowded prison system in which four in five inmates are detained on drug-related charges.

Back in the US, some of the sentences are farcical: many people are given maximum sentences for possessing small amounts of drugs. In 2015 in Texas, 16,000 people were sentenced to time in state jails for possession of less than 1 gram ($^7/_2$ oz) of a drug. The number of those imprisoned in the US for non-violent drug law offences rose from 40,000 in 1980 to more than 500,000 thirty years later – most of whom were not high-level operators and had no prior criminal records.

A

Mandatory minimum prison sentences for drugs (USA, 2015)

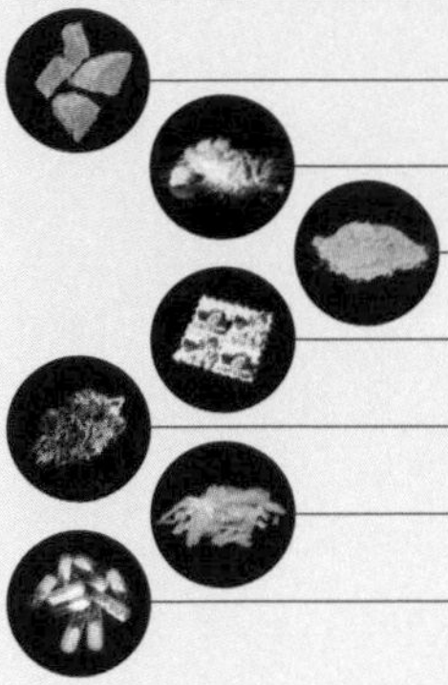

Drug	5 years	10 years
Crack cocaine	28g (1 oz)	280g (10 oz)
Powder cocaine	500g (17⅗ oz)	5,000g (176 oz)
Heroin	100g (3½ oz)	1,000g (35 oz)
LSD	1g (1/25 oz)	10g (⅖ oz)
Marijuana	100,000g (3,527 oz)	1,000,000g (35,274 oz)
Meth (pure)	5g (⅕ oz)	50g (1⅘ oz)
PCP	10g (⅖ oz)	100g (½ oz)

B

Today, in the US, half of the 2 million inmates were jailed for drug-related crimes, resulting in a conveniently constant stream of prisoners for what often amounts to slave labour. These people – often those from Black and ethnic minorities – have been exploited on a mass scale, due to structural racism and ingrained inequality, into dealing drugs from a young age.

But without the spectre of laws preventing drug distribution and use, how would some states and their police forces justify their actions? Academic Noam Chomsky (b. 1928) wrote in *Hopes and Prospects* (2010) that the war on drugs 'served to frighten the population into obedience as domestic policies were being implemented to benefit extreme wealth at the expense of the large majority'. By the end of George W. Bush's (b. 1946) presidency, there were around 40,000 military-style raids annually, mostly for non-violent drug offences. A UN working group has warned that responding to 'the world's drug problem' has been used to justify excessive surveillance and the targeting of people of African descent all over the world, more closely representing a system of racial control than a method to address drug use and trafficking.

A

A   Protester at a rally in
    Washington, DC, in
    June 2013. Drug and
    criminal justice policy
    reform advocates and
    faith and community
    leaders, who organized
    the march, called
    on President Barack
    Obama to end the
    war on drugs 'as a
    pipeline to the mass
    incarceration of Black
    people'.
B   'Cocaine gun' was the
    first teen anti-drugs
    advertising campaign
    by the Partnership for
    a Drug-Free America
    (now known as the
    Partnership to End
    Addiction), created
    in 1987. The award-
    winning adverts ran
    in the *Wall Street
    Journal* and *New
    York Times*.

The apocalyptic rhetoric of international policymakers around drug use has provided cover for states that have committed other human rights violations in the name of drug control. According to Professor Rick Lines in *Drug Control and Human Rights in International Law* (2017), slavery, apartheid, nuclear war and torture are not described in the international conventions as evil. But the UN Single Convention on Narcotic Drugs (1961) asserts that 'addiction to narcotic drugs constitutes a serious evil for the individual and is fraught with social and economic danger to mankind'.

But does the evil not arise as a product of prohibition rather than from the drugs themselves? Some experts maintain that the diversion of money from the drug war to social development issues, alongside regulatory frameworks, would likely solve many of the problems and even bring us closer to a more just world. So why not end the war?

Fundamentally, bureaucracies do not like to admit mistakes and whole institutions have a vested interest in the continuation of the war. 'It's like pest control companies, they only control,' Guillermo Terrazas Villanueva, a Mexican regional spokesperson told Al-Jazeera in 2012. 'If you finish off the pests, you are out of a job. If they finish the drug business, they finish their jobs.'

B

In the absence of a global movement with widespread and/or elite backing, states do not have to seriously account for their actions – despite the growing deadly harms. The question is, how do citizens gain a position of power and challenge the small cliques holding political power?

Others will be unsurprisingly terrified that drug gangs may turn their guns on the police and the military if substantive changes are enacted. But with rising demand and production as the trade grows ever more sophisticated and more difficult to disrupt, zero tolerance policies and reactionary militarization continue to add to the death toll of millions of lives.

A   Weapons and drugs seized from members of the criminal gang Mara Salvatrucha (MS-13) in Honduras, 2021. The group was established in Los Angeles, USA, to protect Salvadoran immigrants from other gangs, and is now frequently referenced by Republican politicians advocating stricter migration controls.

B   A 'no dumping' sign placed in the slums of Rio de Janeiro, Brazil, in February 2018 and signed by the drug-trafficking gang Comando Vermelho, which controls Rio de Janeiro's City of God favela.

C   Members of the Global Commission on Drug Policy (GCDP) – a panel of world leaders and intellectuals – at a press conference in New York, USA in June 2011. They had just published a report calling for the decriminalization of drug use by those who do no harm to others.

D   The GCDP accept a petition at the press conference in June 2011, calling for an end to the war on drugs, to be delivered to the United Nations.

A **zero tolerance** policy means applying the same punishment to all infringements of a law, without consideration of individual circumstance or the level of infringement. The policy is intended to emphasize the importance of the law, and act as a deterrent.

Militarization describes the increasingly military character of drug law enforcement, the result of expanded funding for police and aggressive policies.

The US has resorted to attempting to control the drug trade, effectively favouring certain groups over others, rather than eradicating it. Police forces around the world are now often leading the way in effectively decriminalizing drug use, with many sick of fighting a futile war on the frontlines.

What would happen if you prevented hundreds of billions of dollars from being earned by organized crime networks and terrorist organizations, and helped stop gangs fighting over the cash while innocent people get caught in the crossfire? And why haven't policymakers made any true attempt to do so?

A

A man standing at the bar scratches his cocaine-coloured nose, glancing furtively from side to side, while two women jive to the rhythm of the music nearby and sweat profusely as their pupils dilate from the MDMA they have taken. In between the bar and the dancefloor is a young man making his way round almost everyone in the club to ask whether they want drugs. 'Pills, ket, coke?' he asks. This scene repeats itself every day in hundreds of cities across the world. So what would change through legalizing drugs in nightclubs where it is already *de facto* legal?

Perhaps clubs where drugs could be consumed could not serve alcohol (due to heightened risks from mixing), and drug harm-reduction services could be present to prevent contaminated and deadly substances from being sold. The only fundamental difference would be that a criminal dealer, who may well be in and out of trouble with the law, would not be there, but a nearby set of pharmacy-like shops – which would close at a certain time – could supply the demand. The tax income would be reinvested into harm reduction and education, with reparations paid to communities that have suffered in the name of the drug war. You may raise your eyebrows at the simplicity of this suggestion, but take a moment to ponder how the idea that the Earth moves around the sun was once radical heresy, homosexuality was considered evil and smoking believed not harmful to health.

The evidence in favour of wholesale reform is approaching the point where anti-drugs dogma is impossible to uphold. Hard-line anti-drugs statements from politicians are becoming laughable, even to the average citizen. Some opposition politicians are even mustering the courage to suggest that it would be safer to sell drugs in a regulated market than leave gangsters to sell dangerous products in a free-for-all. These common-sense arguments are sometimes dismissed as 'dangerously irresponsible' policies that could lead to 'social catastrophe'. Moreover, they fear legalization could undermine the desired message that while drinking whisky is okay, drug use is wrong.

A   Stoner icon and rapper, Wiz Khalifa, performs at a nightclub in Las Vegas, USA, in June 2021. People often openly smoke cannabis at his shows.
B   A woman takes cocaine in a toilet. Mixing cocaine and alcohol can spawn a separate addiction to cocaethylene – the chemical created by combining the two.

B

DECRIMINALIZING AND REGULATING DRUG USE

105

Growing numbers of people across the world favour progressive and human rights-centred approaches that depart from ideology and morality. These people have not, however, reached such numbers as to form a critical mass that could force political accountability for figures manipulated by cartels, banks and market forces strongly influenced by illegal drug flows.

Three of the countries most adversely affected by the drug war – Mexico, Colombia and Guatemala – have pressed for prohibitionist policies to be re-evaluated globally, and alternatives such as decriminalization and legal regulation of drug markets to be considered. UN agencies dropped their much-derided goal of achieving a drug-free world and, in a joint statement in 2019, quietly called for decriminalization and the repeal of 'punitive laws' criminalizing personal drug use that are proven to have negative public health outcomes. One agency has even noted the tragi-comic irony that our increasingly materialistic, consumerist world leaves ever more people craving drugs. At least 30 countries have already effectively decriminalized the use of many drugs, with some – most notably Portugal but also the Czech Republic – doing so for all drugs. Scotland is also inching towards such a policy. A revolution is quietly proceeding, with policies sometimes relatively unannounced, perhaps fearing pushback.

A

A A woman smokes a joint during a 2021 demonstration demanding the legalization of marijuana for recreational use in Bogotá, Colombia. Major drug reforms are increasingly being debated in the country, with senators considering whether to regulate cocaine – though the measure is unlikely to pass.

B Chart showing the drug death rate in Portugal against the rest of Europe in 2020. The death rate In Portugal plummeted after the country decriminalized drug use and massively expanded treatment and outreach services for people with dependencies, although the rate has since risen. Campaigners suggest this demonstrates the limits of a model that still leaves supply in the hands of organized crime.

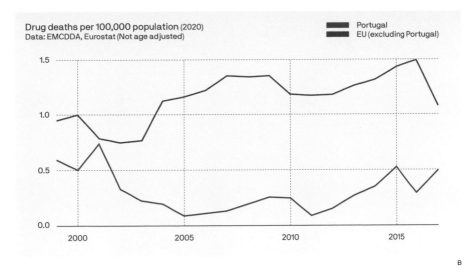

Drug deaths per 100,000 population (2020)
Data: EMCDDA, Eurostat (Not age adjusted)

Portugal
EU (excluding Portugal)

B

In 2001, Portugal abolished criminal penalties for drug use in an effort to move away from a punitive approach and reallocate resources to healthcare services. People found in possession of personal amounts of drugs are referred to a 'Drug Addiction Dissuasion Commission' ahead of referral to education or treatment programmes. Drug misuse in the country exploded in the 1970s after it transitioned to a democracy and opened up to the world. The country was ill-equipped to deal with the influx, and drug dependency blighted a wide cross-section of society, unlike in some other countries where the worst harms are more visibly confined to working-class communities, despite vast hidden harms within more privileged communities.

People with dependencies are now sent for counselling and other forms of treatment following a mass national rollout and serious investment. Problematic drug use has fallen, after at least 1% of the population was dependent on drugs. Just 22 people died related to drugs in 2015, down from 369 in 1999, though it rose to 51 in 2017. New cases of HIV infection among those who inject drugs fell from 1,482 to 78 in the same period. Outreach work is bold, with public health officials going to marginalized parts of the country to offer help. The architect of the policies, Dr João Goulão, has said, 'The biggest effect has been to allow the stigma of drug addiction to fall, to let people speak clearly and to pursue professional help without fear.'

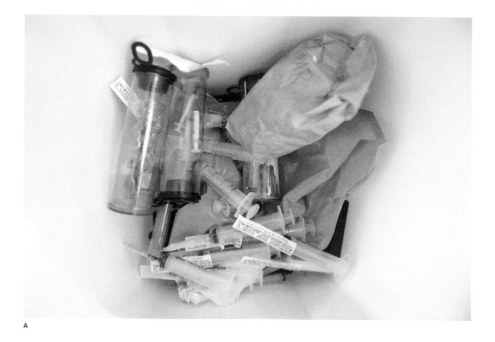

A

Portugal followed the lead of the Czech Republic, which decriminalized drug use and personal possession in the 1990s and introduced harm-reduction policies in swift response to rising heroin use. This approach appears to have prevented crisis levels of deaths there.

Needle exchange programmes and opioid substitute programmes were rolled out in places at risk, treatment centres had a low threshold of availability – you did not have to be dependent on drugs – and outreach programmes accessed hidden at-risk populations. HIV prevalence among those injecting drugs remained low, and those found to have committed non-violent, drug-related offences were not jailed – sparing society the enormous costs. Meanwhile, a new crime relating to 'spreading addiction' was legislated for to address predatory dealing. In 1999, drug possession for 'amounts larger than small' was re-criminalized, though decriminalization remained beneath this threshold. But after an assessment found that it had no deterrent effect on drug misuse and led police to waste more than €5,000 on each case, it was rolled back in 2010. The country still has one of the lowest rates of drug-related deaths in the EU.

Though it stopped short of decriminalizing all drugs, Switzerland may have avoided a major public health crisis amid high rates of HIV by rolling out prescribed heroin for people with dependencies in 1994. They had opened the world's first formally sanctioned, supervised injection facility eight years earlier. Health outcomes significantly improved, while associated crime plummeted as the most vulnerable no longer had to beg or commit crimes to maintain their dependency. Drug dealers had previously been highly visible thanks to an open drug scene, but the compassionate policy did away with much of what was described as an economy of misery and squalor.

Heroin-assisted treatment is also being tested tentatively, or is in place, in the Netherlands, Germany, Spain, Denmark, the UK and Canada, where it marginalizes the criminal market, provides sterile equipment and means people do not have to steal, beg or sell their bodies to prevent crippling withdrawal symptoms.

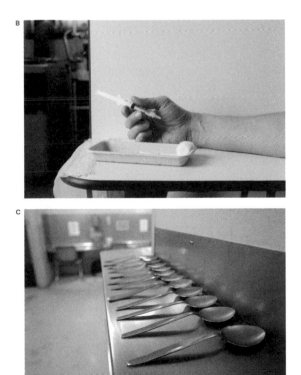

B

C

A   A bin containing used needles at a needle exchange facility in Stockholm, Sweden, in 2014. The country criminalized illegal drug use in 1988 and within two decades had a drug-related death rate four times the EU average.

B   A trial in a clinic in south London, UK, in 2007, testing the effectiveness of pharmaceutical heroin, known as diamorphine, for stopping street heroin use. Clients received the drug twice daily, seven days a week, along with a range of psychiatric and social support.

C   A drug consumption room in Bern, Switzerland, one of the first cities to introduce such facilities two decades ago. People can come with their own drugs and inject themselves at the centre more safely than on the street.

Until the UK bowed to US pressure in the 1970s and vastly downscaled what was known as the British System from the late 1920s, hundreds of people with heroin dependencies were able to access it on prescription through a doctor. They were able to live otherwise normal lives and uphold jobs while maintaining a congenial relationship with their doctor without needing to interact with dangerous criminals. Education was provided, with honest guidance on safer doses and what to do in the event of overdoses, and a violent illegal market – with its predatory dealers – was relatively unheard of (though it predated the explosion of heroin production and deindustrialization).

Other countries resisted pressure for a crackdown. Drugs have long been *de facto* decriminalized in the Netherlands. The country's *gedoogbeleid* policy of tolerating possession for personal use has made cannabis smoking effectively legal. The Netherlands famously allows coffee shops to supply cannabis (though paradoxically it has long been illegal to supply the shops). However, the rate of consumption there is lower than or equal to that of neighbouring countries. In the US, in states where cannabis has been legalized, usage of the drug among teenagers has decreased, or remained the same, although it has risen in people aged over 26.

A

The **British System** was an informal arrangement in which doctors in the UK, mostly in London, prescribed free heroin to people dependent on the drug.

Coffee shops in the Netherlands allow the legal sale and consumption of cannabis.

A   A street in downtown Amsterdam, Netherlands, where coffee shops have long provided locals and tourists alike with a wide array of cannabis products.
B   A man calls for the legalization of cocaine during a protest in Vancouver, Canada, May 2021. The city passed a motion to ask the federal government to decriminalize the possession of illicit drugs in the city.

B

Decriminalization does not tackle the question of supply, however. Many have argued that the very fact some drugs are extremely harmful yet in demand means that states have the responsibility to regulate them and not leave their provision to the world's largest criminal commodity market.

In Portugal, often incorrectly held up as a seemingly perfect model of drug liberalization, it is claimed that some authority figures are deeply complicit in drug trafficking. Meanwhile, in the Netherlands, the state has been cracking down on growers, forcing the country's famous coffee shops, visited by millions from around the world each year, to source their produce from organized crime groups in step with increasing violence. A legal production trial was approved in 2021 to supply the coffee shops.

Regulation in much of the world has been confined to cannabis, with change driven variously by commercial incentives, social justice and sheer pragmatism. Cannabis has been completely legalized in Canada, Uruguay and 18 US states, with Mexico, Switzerland, Germany, South Africa and Jamaica seemingly waiting in the wings. Dozens more US states allow medicinal use.

A

B

A   Decriminalize Nature
    DC is a political
    campaign to remove
    criminal penalties for
    many psychedelics.
    The group is not
    in favour of legal
    regulation, however,
    as they do not believe
    the state has that right.
B   The Decriminalize
    Nature Minneapolis
    campaign stresses
    that removing criminal
    penalties would help
    improve the physical,
    mental and emotional
    health of communities.
C   People smoke and
    rate cannabis strains
    during a meeting of
    a cannabis association
    on the Spanish island
    of Fuerteventura in
    January 2014. Spain
    has some of Europe's
    most liberal cannabis
    laws.

Cannabis **social clubs** are spaces, most notably across Spain, where members bring home-grown weed to sell at affordable prices; though some are increasingly commercial.

After research was grudgingly sanctioned, the evidence base for the therapeutic, breakthrough potential of many illegal drugs has become increasingly impressive amid scant developments in psychiatric medicine. It appears MDMA and psilocybin could receive FDA approval for certain treatments in the coming years. Decriminalize Nature, which argues humans have an unalienable right to develop their own relationship with natural plants, persuaded US authorities in half a dozen municipalities, including Washington, DC, to decriminalize all plant-based psychedelics. In 2021, the Californian Senate passed a bill to legalize the possession and social sharing of psychedelics. Oregon is decriminalizing the possession of personal amounts of all drugs, while psilocybin therapy has been licensed and the state's health department has been tasked with licensing therapists to administer them. 'A civilization that supports the adult individual's right to utilize chemical catalysts for self-discovery and spiritual communion might advance to a more mature and stable state,' writes Daniel Pinchbeck in a new introduction to *The Psychedelic Experience* (2017) by Timothy Leary.

In Uruguay, the first country to legalize cannabis for non-medical use in 2013 despite relative public opposition, there are three legal channels – social clubs, home-growing and state-run pharmacies, which sell in unbranded packaging at prices fixed by the government to registered adult buyers.

This appears to have helped marginalize organized crime groups formerly operating in the cannabis market, though an illegal market remains to supply non-Uruguayans who remain shut out from the legal market. There is also a lack of legal availability in some parts of the country, and concerns that former cannabis offenders have not had their sentences expunged.

Although they do not necessarily save lives, cannabis social clubs are also an entirely sensible approach. Across Europe, there are around 2,000 such places, mostly in Spain.

Some adhere to a model where designated members bring their home-grown cannabis, which is sold at non-commercial rates. The members-only clubs are relaxed places with pool tables, video games and table tennis tables. It is almost utopian, although the lack of availability of low-THC products is a cause for concern. Cannabis enthusiasts have set up similar spaces in Germany, Italy and the UK, some to explicitly test the desire of police to enforce laws that they are increasingly wary of.

C

A

B

A   Employees place mite sachets on cannabis plants at a growing facility in Ontario, Canada, in July 2019. Legal cannabis sales in Ontario overtook those made through the illegal market for the first time ever between July and September 2020 after prices were cut and unlicensed dispensaries were raided. Annual national sales were about $2 billion, compared to $17.5 billion in the US, where cannabis remained illegal at the federal level.

B   Cannabis plants hang in a curing shed at a craft growing operation in British Columbia, Canada, November 2018. In the first major industrialized country to legalize recreational cannabis, can cottage industries be developed in the face of looming corporate dominance?

C   Customers wait outside the 'Sweet Relief' cannabis store in Northport, Maine, on the first day of legal sales in October 2020, after it became the ninth US state to sanction legal recreational use following a public vote.

That said, in Barcelona, Spain, the establishments are facing serious regulatory pressure amid concerns over 'weed tourism' and organized crime involvement after some went rogue and abandoned the original small club, non-profit ethos. Authorities nonetheless acknowledge that the model has reduced street dealing and consumption.

Time after time, more pragmatic approaches have been shunned due to fears of criminal involvement. Why not marginalize the criminals once and for all? Some countries are attempting to do so.

Justin Trudeau's (b. 1971) government in Canada was elected in 2015 on a central campaign promise to legalize and regulate a non-medical adult cannabis market – a pledge they honoured three years later.

However, there have been pitfalls, mirrored in California. Due to start-up costs and administrative red tape, it has taken time for the legal market to eventually comprise half of sales. But the trajectory is away from illegal sellers. There were just 257 pardons for cannabis-related offences, not full expungements, in the first year of the legal market – highlighting the need not just to legalize the drug but to expunge now legal activities from historic criminal records. There is now growing momentum for total drug decriminalization among some state governments.

In the US, cannabis legalization came first in Colorado after a public vote in favour of the move, which was enacted in 2012. People were henceforth allowed to grow up to six plants and commercial vendors opened too. In Massachusetts, people with former cannabis convictions have been supported to work within the cannabis market via the state's pioneering equity schemes after legalization in 2018 following a referendum, mirroring similar schemes in Illinois and California. Recognizing that the market should not be handed directly to corporations, policymakers sought the recruitment of people from areas most impacted by prohibition.

C

A

A   An employee arranges
    a display of cannabis at
    a dispensary in Oakland,
    California, March 2020.
    The state's 'shelter-
    in-place' Covid order
    allowed people in the
    most populous US state
    to leave their homes for
    essential items such as
    groceries and medicine,
    including cannabis.

B   This is what legal cocaine
    packaging could one
    day look like, according
    to campaigners from
    Transform Drug Policy
    Foundation.

White-owned venture capital dominates the market in most states. Changes have also been applied unevenly. Research in the 18 states that have legalized recreational cannabis has found that it does not increase use, but racial discrimination persists, with Black people almost twice as likely as white people to be arrested for related offences. In Chicago, cannabis smoking in social housing is banned and there have been no policies for the hiring of former drug dealers – though 20,000 have been pardoned as part of half a million expungements statewide. New York, San Francisco and California are among those who have moved similarly.

Though cannabis remains illegal at the federal level, this has been a locally-led, bottom-up revolution thanks to direct democracy ballot initiatives that do not exist in many places across the world. Meanwhile, products containing the non-psychoactive part of cannabis, CBD, now proliferate in the high streets of many countries and hedge funds have invested billions in firms that appear to be waiting for further cannabis liberalization. We are past the point of no return.

So, what could a highly regulated legalized stimulant market look like?

According to Steve Rolles, from Transform Drug Policy Foundation, it would almost certainly lead to a more diverse range of products and strengths being available as part of a three-tier model depending on product risk. People would also think twice about their consumption after knowing the health risks. Pilot schemes would assess the efficacy of licensed pharmacies selling rationed amounts of MDMA, cocaine and amphetamine to registered members of the public who had passed driver's licence-style courses. In addition to a powdered form, drugs could come in dose-sized tablets, slow-releasing capsules and lozenges. These proposals are the basis of the model described in a cocaine regulation bill now being debated in the Colombian Senate. Depending on the risk, some drugs would remain prohibited for sale in the expectation that demand for them would drastically reduce thanks to the reforms.

B

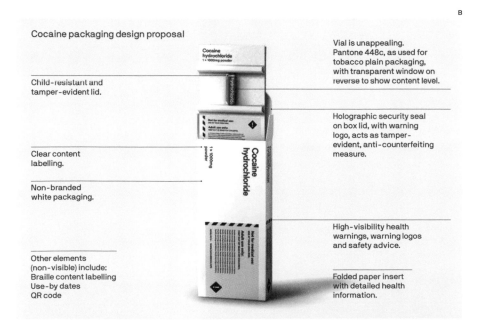

Cocaine packaging design proposal

Child-resistant and tamper-evident lid.

Clear content labelling.

Non-branded white packaging.

Other elements (non-visible) include:
Braille content labelling
Use-by dates
QR code

Vial is unappealing. Pantone 448c, as used for tobacco plain packaging, with transparent window on reverse to show content level.

Holographic security seal on box lid, with warning logo, acts as tamper-evident, anti-counterfeiting measure.

High-visibility health warnings, warning logos and safety advice.

Folded paper insert with detailed health information.

Elsewhere, heroin would be prescribed to those with addictions. Columbia University professor Carl Hart, who uses heroin recreationally, has also advocated for it to be available for sale. In this imagined world, trained vendors enforcing a code of practice while providing tailored health advice would work face-to-face with consumers, whose details would be held on a computerized database subject to strict protection laws. As opposed to almost every criminal market, cross-selling would not be tolerated. You would not be offered cocaine if you were buying amphetamine, for instance, and neither would the former be padded out by the latter.

Separate shops could be established for psychedelics such as magic mushrooms, LSD, 2CB and DMT, acting under the same constraints. Already, in the Netherlands, so-called 'smart shops' sell a variety of legal drugs, such as psilocybin truffles, LSA and salvia. Assistants aid customers with their shopping, asking about health complaints, what they have in their system and what experience they wish to achieve.

A

B

LSA is a natural hallucinogen found in vines and fungi that is structurally similar to LSD.

Salvia is a fast-acting hallucinogenic drug from the mint family that can cause sometimes terrifying distortions of time and space with opiate effects.

Head shops sell products related to the consumption of cannabis – such as pipes, bongs and grinders – but not the drug itself.

A   Magic mushrooms at a smart shop in Amsterdam, Netherlands, 2007.
B   A range of cannabis-infused products, including chocolate and tea, for sale in Amsterdam, Netherlands.
C   Unbranded, drab-coloured cigarette packaging with health warning, 2017.
D   Menthol pods from electronic cigarette company Juul.

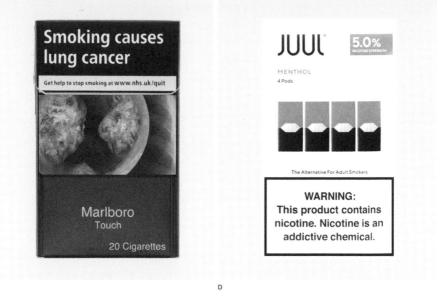

C   D

Unlike at so-called head shops, the sale of drugs would not be commercialized and advertising would be prohibited. A robust regulatory framework would need to be in place prior to the arrival of products – which would be sold either by a state monopoly or non-profit enterprises – to market. State monopolies and tightly controlled structures similar to those governing the prescription of certain pharmaceuticals would be policed by a truly independent government agency. Prices would be fixed and there could be no opportunity for profiteering, although private enterprise could play a role in transporting and producing the products. A state monopoly would be preferable. The lessons from alcohol and tobacco sales have to be learned: a liberalized market cannot be trusted to safeguard people's health, in much the same way as an illegal market, since problematic use offers greater profits than infrequent consumption. The drugs would be plainly packaged with health risks and a helpline for problematic use. New York allows cannabis consumption where tobacco can be smoked and it seems only liberal policies would prevent the continuance of marginalized people being targeted.

It is not unfeasible that parts of the night-time economy would shift from a business model focusing on alcohol sales, to one of stimulant-friendliness – providing experiences such as massages and high-end juices to those who arrive at their establishment with their own drugs, to make up for the shortfall from booze sales.

Regulation done properly should eventually lead to reduced prices for many drugs. If non-profit mechanisms were not safeguarded, then more powerful enterprises than those currently involved could have an interest in fuelling dependency to drive profit. Thus, there are well-founded fears that, without robust and assertive state structures, gambling liberalization and the opioid epidemic could repeat themselves.

Any legal drug market would require an age limit, which would inevitably create a demand for a criminal market. It remains to be seen whether it would mimic the small illegal market for alcohol, where sympathetic elders buy it on behalf of children. Still, some experts believe that even if consumption was to rise – as cannabis use has done slightly in Canada and Uruguay – it would, among other reasons, be better for public health since quality would be assured.

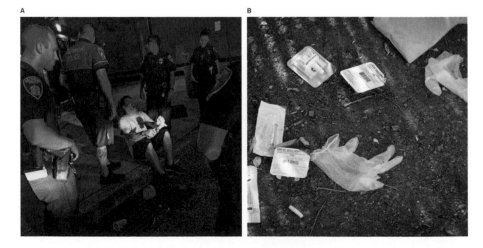

A

B

C

D

Kevin Sabet (b. 1979), a former drug advisor to successive US governments, has claimed that legalization would increase dependency and normalize childhood use – though this has not materialized with regards to cannabis. It is not implausible that tensions between states or corporations would be inflamed as they wrestled for access to each other's markets to sell drugs. The cartel skirmishes and street violence of today could reach new extremes. Yet it is perhaps more likely that criminal groups would simply shift into fresh enterprises, or merge with the legitimate economy. The loss of cannabis profits has seen Latin American crime groups move further into illegal mining, logging and controlling the supply of alcohol.

States also fear that reducing penalties could corrode respect for authorities and the law, signalling that drug use, and by extension other crimes, is acceptable. Arguably, the rule of law has already been irrevocably eroded due to the inequitable application of drug laws. The effectiveness of any future policies would also be influenced by pre-existing cultures of compliance, taxpaying and law enforcement. Some believe that violence is inextricably linked to the use of some drugs due to the way they make you feel, not just the criminal distribution rings.

Crack cocaine, for instance, can bring on paranoia and increase aggressiveness, often linking it to domestic violence. Even if crack cocaine was not sold in a regulated market, there is nothing stopping anyone from simply making it from cocaine powder. A prudent regulatory framework would ensure other controversial drugs such as GHB could solely be sold in individual low doses with appropriate safeguards.

It is not inevitable, however, that drug use would rise. It is already at record-high levels – prohibition has not prevented that. Advocates of stricter drug policies point to drug-related violence, but it is also fuelled by a number of other factors, not least alcohol and a lack of effective treatment services. What we need is a compassionate and pragmatic system to help people when they are in need. And people are not waiting for change. Already, the lives of dependent people who use drugs are being saved in Drug Consumption Rooms (DCRs), also known as Overdose Prevention Centres (OPCs), across at least 11 countries (Canada, Australia and others in Western Europe), where people can take their illegally obtained drugs in a hygienic space under supervision.

A

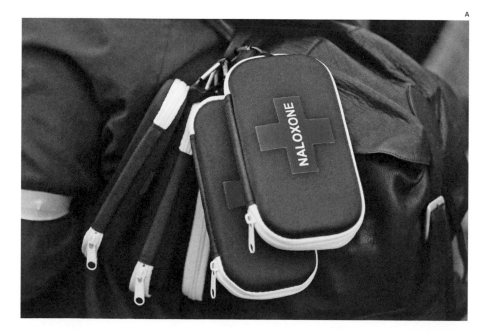

A   The Toronto Overdose
    Prevention society holds
    a march in October 2018,
    ending with a vigil at Moss
    Park overdose prevention
    site. It advocates use of the
    overdose antidote naloxone
    carry kits, which for a number
    of years have reportedly
    saved innumerable lives.

B/C Activist Peter Krykant,
    formerly dependent on
    heroin, established a drug
    consumption van in Glasgow,
    Scotland, in 2020. Inside
    people can inject drugs more
    safely, under supervision.
    It is one attempt to get a
    grip on Scotland's spiralling
    drug death crisis.

B

C

GHB is a central nervous system chemical depressant known as the 'date rape' drug due to its ability to make people pass out quickly.

There has never been a fatal overdose in any of the facilities – with thousands of deaths saved by the provision of naloxone and other basic health interventions. Needle sharing is also eliminated through provision of clean injecting equipment. A gateway to drug treatment is offered to people from hard-to-reach communities, along with referral to other healthcare and social services. Drugs can also be tested for contamination and purity, often leading to the quality of drugs available locally improving significantly.

In Denmark, pressure from campaigners taking direct action and providing mobile DCR support to people dependent on drugs from an out-of-service ambulance led to changes in the law to allow such facilities to operate legally. Up to 10,000 syringes were found each week in Copenhagen's former meatpacking district Vesterbro, where there was a historic open drug scene, until the DCR opened in 2012. People who inject drugs were soon shielded from public view and taken much greater care of. The number of needles fell below 1,000 within a year.

A MDMA pills tested in 2019/2020 by KnowYourStuffNZ in Aotearoa, New Zealand, where drug checking at festivals and public clinics is legal. The quantity of MDMA in similar-looking pills varied from year to year.

B Harm-reduction organizations can issue people with kits to test their drugs at home for purity. This leads to more educated drug use as people are aware of what their substance actually contains and can modify their behaviour accordingly.

A

It is not just on the streets where law-and-order focused drug policy kills. Yet new approaches are also emerging within clubs and festivals. Some events in Europe have drug testing to analyse for adulteries and impurities, along with personalized health warnings delivered in one-on-one sessions where the purity of the drug is revealed. Urban testing is also offered in countries such as the Netherlands. Research suggests the measures are life-saving. The vast majority of people using the services say they have never received specialized drug education before. Warnings are issued publicly as well, via social media alerts for example, when dangerous substances are discovered, in the absence of similar information from the state.

But there remains widespread resistance to their introduction due to a perception that it encourages drug-taking; much the same as the argument that preceded needle exchange trials, and many other harm-reduction interventions. There is no evidence that testing services increase drug use.

In the face of powerful interests favouring drug prohibition, it may seem obvious why so many politicians, some of whom take drugs, only support reform once they are out of office. Very few get into politics motivated by drug policy but some do realize the chaos wrought by prohibition in the streets, in courts largely dealing with petty crimes driven by drug dependency and across the world. They tend to claim not to have had the opportunity to act.

While drug policy is still seen as a divisive issue that risks alienating voters, reform is increasingly becoming an asset rather than a liability for politicians. Ultimately, the inevitability of demand must be accepted along with the failure and the tremendous costs of prohibition. There is a clear trend towards decriminalization and harm reduction, but campaigners say it does not go far enough as the harms of the illegal trade remain.

Further change is on the horizon. The WHO has at least now removed cannabis from the most restrictive category of the 1961 Single Convention, thus acknowledging it has a medical utility. In 2021 the International Narcotics Control Board, the implementation body monitoring the UN drug treaties, called 'for reflection on possible alternative and additional agreements, instruments and forms of cooperation to respond to the changing nature and magnitude of the global drug problem'.

B

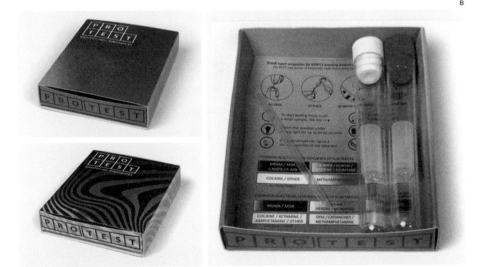

A

Ghana has vastly reduced penalties for drug use, marking it out as progressive for the region's standards, and its government has told the UN that 'the greatest harms of prohibition are high levels of crime, corruption and violence as well as massive illicit markets'. Norway's centre-right governing party attempted to decriminalize, though it was voted down by liberals who claimed it would encourage youth drug use. In Thailand, in 2021, the plant-based painkiller kratom was decriminalized and it was announced that 121 people convicted of possession or sale would be released immediately.

In 2019 a judge in Mexico granted two people the right to use cocaine in what campaigners hailed as 'another step in the fight to construct alternative drug policies', but policies for drug arrests to be replaced by the enforcement of treatment, such as attendance of a detox programme, are poorly understood by authorities and not properly implemented by police. The country's president has also suggested referenda on the legalization of some drugs, especially those with medicinal qualities, to bring 'peace and tranquillity' to Mexico.

The UN secretary general is now António Guterres (b. 1949), who was Portuguese prime minister when Portugal decriminalized drugs. As more countries follow this path, the case for regulation will become inescapable. Even the US is under pressure to abandon the war from dissenting voices within Congress. Laws and their enforcement only have a limited effect on levels of drug use, even if they evidently have a profoundly negative effect on the level of drug-related harms. Reformers argue society is obligated to make drug markets and drug-taking, a central part of the human experience, as safe as possible.

A   A nurse dispenses medicine to patients in a rehabilitation programme in Thailand, August 2017. Thailand launched a harm-reduction programme to tackle drug dependence after admitting the country's war on drugs had not been won as the number of drug addicts and drug-related offences had only increased. They are increasingly treating people who use drugs as patients and sending them to rehab instead of prison.

B   A woman dances at a full moon party in Koh Phangan, Thailand, in March 2004. Thousands flock to the all-night beach parties where revellers commonly drink magic mushroom smoothies prepared and sold by locals.

C   Laughing gas – the nitrous oxide used to whip cream and inflate balloons – is breathed in at a party in Bristol, UK, in 2010. It is demonized in the media as hippy crack, due to the shortlived euphoria it brings.

Conclusion

A

A   A cannabis enthusiast celebrates cannabis legalization in Toronto, Canada, in October 2018. Canada was the first G7 state to make the move at a federal level. The country's companies are now well placed to benefit from a global green rush as others increasingly relax laws and look to legalize.

B   Russian police guard a storage area in Bryansk Region, Russia, in September 2021, where a batch of soon-to-be-destroyed cocaine is kept. The facility is intended for destroying all forms of drugs that have been seized or confiscated.

Drugs are being legalized around the world, with different countries at various stages.

Regardless of the law, drugs are already consumed and misused in abundance. Use, production and sales are rising rapidly as the global middle class expands, despite futile and now-abandoned efforts spearheaded by the US and the UN to create a 'drug-free world'. Humans have an insatiable appetite for drugs; they are all around us and they will never be eradicated from society. Even pandemic border closures failed to significantly affect markets due to the sheer scale of the demand and resultant profit motive.

Prohibition and the waging of a war against drugs has done more harm to people than the drugs themselves, and there is a growing acceptance that repression cannot erase humankind's innate desire to explore altered states. If society believes there is something intrinsically immoral in altering consciousness, then alcohol and tobacco should be banned. Pragmatism rules this out in the majority of the world though, and drug use can never be suffocated. Given the historic failures to reduce demand and restrict supply of drugs, it is time for a new, compassionate and pragmatic approach.

Only through regulation, and the sensible legal provision of drugs, does it seem that states could remove billions of dollars from the pockets of organized crime groups who challenge their power, cause misery and plague institutions with corruption, and instead collect gargantuan tax revenues, which could go towards education, intervention, treatment and harm reduction. Growing research suggests this would represent good overall value for money.

B

State companies would be required to provide better-quality products at competitive prices. This should not be difficult as the prices are vastly inflated due to prohibition. Of course, even the most advanced democracies are not immune to corruption and cronyism, but surely states are better placed to manage these billions of dollars.

Regulating sales of heroin and opium, cocaine, MDMA and amphetamines under strict licensing regimes while providing a looser but non-commercial regime of various stringencies for cannabis, ketamine, magic mushrooms, LSD, methadone and the less harmful NPSs appears to be the only way to get a grip on the public health crisis engulfing the world. Anyone who really wants them as it stands can buy them anyway.

Regulation would also vastly improve the quality of drugs and eliminate risks of contamination, mis-selling and lack of known strength and purity. It would provide a greater range so that people would have a choice between different drugs – including less potent and slower-acting options instead of the most rapid-hit preparations that tend to dominate street markets. Other drugs would be prescribed.

A

B

NPSs, or new psychoactive substances, are specifically designed to avoid legal definitions of illegality by altering chemical structures slightly.

Regulation in Mexico, Afghanistan, Colombia and other countries devastated by the futile war, which they have financed to the tune of billions gifted and borrowed largely from the US, could potentially transform their economies for the better.

There are concerns that inadequate regulation could open Pandora's box. It is possible the cartels and drug gangs would seek to expand into other forms of criminal activity such as counterfeiting and extortion.

Free market legalization and an absence of controls could be even more dangerous than the current anarchy, with corporations able to aggressively market poorly regulated products to impressionable young people. Much as the alcohol and tobacco industries have done in the past with devastating impacts. Rising numbers of people may behave obnoxiously, emboldened by drugs, as drunks throughout society do already. Perhaps corporations would even go to war with each other over the lucrative profits in prospect. Or they could encourage doctors to prescribe certain drugs, the deadly consequences of which the opioid crisis in the US has shown, with increasing restrictions on prescriptions only forcing people towards the black market.

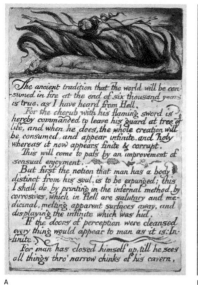

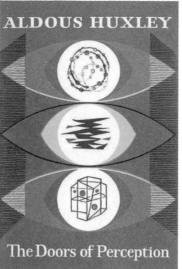

A/B *The Doors of Perception* is an autobiographical book written in 1954 by author and philosopher Aldous Huxley, describing his psychedelic experience under the influence of mescaline – in which he recalls the 'purely aesthetic' and 'sacramental visions'. The title was taken from William Blake's *The Marriage of Heaven and Hell*, published in 1790.

C Smiley, ecstasy and acid badges at an acid house party at Heaven nightclub in London, UK, 1988.

A   B

But this speculation is no reason to maintain the status quo. Instead, it is an argument for ensuring that responsible regulation follows a legalization process, ideally using non-commercial models and strict controls over pricing and products to ensure private forces would not act in the interests of profit rather than public health. Even a state-controlled model has obvious flaws and risks of exploitation. But we already have experience of what good and bad practice in drugs regulation looks like from the many legal drugs already available in shops and pharmacies, and there is no reason why a new, more responsible model for other currently illegal drugs could not be formulated.

An international commission of prominent medical experts has said that the current superficially tough drug policies lead to crime, violence, deaths and the spread of diseases such as HIV and hepatitis, while harming health and human rights. Drug use has not been curbed. The war on drugs is a generational disaster of epic proportions, corrupting democratic institutions and societies, fuelling drug-related violence and single-handedly bringing criminal justice systems to the point of collapse, while allowing the US and its allies to fight a mutating, neo-imperialist war, which has only created ever greater chaos and suffering as it mutates outside of the US to China and Russia, now the two main protagonists as the US ironically spearheads progressive reforms at home.

The UNODC has long acknowledged its own failure in that global drug control efforts have had a dramatic unintended consequence: the creation of a criminal market of 'staggering proportions'. It understands organized crime is a threat to security and that criminal groups possess the power to both destabilize and corrupt societies, economies and governments – largely thanks to the value of the illegal drug business. 'The only reasonable policy is to open other, better doors in the hope of inducing men and women to exchange their old bad habits for new and less harmful ones,' Huxley argues in *The Doors of Perception* (1954).

It is not so much a war on drugs but a war on people. Human desire and market forces dictate that the war could never be won. It is time to deal with reality and responsibly regulate.

c

Further Reading

Alexander, Bruce, *The Globalization of Addiction: A Study in Poverty of the Spirit* (Oxford: Oxford University Press, 2010)

Berridge, Virginia, *Demons: Our Changing Attitudes to Alcohol, Tobacco and Drugs* (Oxford: Oxford University Press, 2013)

Bowden, Charles, *Murder City: Ciudad Juárez and the Global Economy's New Killing Fields* (New York, NY: Nation Books, 2010)

Branson, Richard, *Ending the War on Drugs* (London: Virgin Books, 2016)

Bullough, Oliver, *Moneyland: Why Thieves and Crooks Now Rule the World and How to Take it Back* (London: Profile Books, 2018)

Daly, Max and Steve Sampson, *Narcomania: How Britain Got Hooked on Drugs* (London: Windmill, 2013)

Davenport-Hines, Richard, *The Pursuit of Oblivion: A Global History of Narcotics* (London: Weidenfeld & Nicolson, 2001)

Evans, Peter, Rueschemeyer, Dietrich and Skocpol, Theda (eds), *Bringing the State Back In* (Cambridge: Cambridge University Press, 1985)

Galeano, Eduardo, *Open Veins of Latin America* (New York, NY: Monthly Review Press, 1971)

Hari, Johann, *Chasing the Scream: The First and Last Days of the War on Drugs* (London: Bloomsbury, 2016)

Hart, Carl, *Drug Use for Grown-Ups: Chasing Liberty in the Land of Fear* (New York, NY: Penguin, 2021)

Huxley, Aldous, *The Doors of Perception* (New York, NY: Harper & Brothers, 1954)

Jay, Mike, *High Society: Mind-Altering Drugs in History and Culture* (London: Thames & Hudson, 2012)

Jay, Mike, *Mescaline: A Global History of the First Psychedelic* (New Haven, CT: Yale University Press, 2019)

Johnson, Graham, *The Cartel: The Inside Story of Britain's Biggest Drug Gang* (Edinburgh: Mainstream, 2013)

Klein, Axel, *Drugs and the World* (London: Reaktion, 2008)

Koram, Kojo (ed.), *The War on Drugs and the Global Colour Line* (London: Pluto Press, 2019)

Leary, Timothy, Ralph Metzner and Richard Alpert, *The Psychedelic Experience: A Manual Based on the Tibetan Book of the Dead* (New Hyde Park, NY: University Books, 1964)

LeBlanc, Nicole, *Random Family: Love, Drugs, Trouble and Coming of Age in the Bronx* (New York, NY: Scribner, 2003)

Letcher, Andy, *Shroom: The Cultural History of the Magic Mushroom* (London: Faber and Faber, 2006)

Levine, Michael, *The Big White Lie: The Deep Cover Operation that Exposed the CIA Sabotage of the Drug War* (New York, NY: Thunder's Mouth Press, 1993)

Loewenstein, Antony, *Pills, Powder and Smoke: Inside the Bloody War on

Drugs (Brunswick, Victoria; Minneapolis, Minnesota: Scribe Publications, 2019)

Lovell, Julia, *The Opium War: Drugs, Dreams and the Making of China* (London: Picador, 2011)

Marks, Howard, *Mr Nice* (London: Vintage, 1998)

Maté, Gabor, *In the Realm of Hungry Ghosts: Close Encounters with Addiction* (Toronto: Vintage Canada, 2012)

Mitchell, Peter R. and John Schoeffel (eds), *Understanding Power: The Indispensable Chomsky* (London: Vintage, 2003)

Nutt, David, *Drink? The New Science of Alcohol and Your Health* (London: Yellow Kite, 2020)

Nutt, David, *Drugs Without the Hot Air: Minimizing the Harms of Illegal and Legal Drugs* (Cambridge: UIT Cambridge, 2012)

Ohler, Norman, *Blitzed: Drugs in Nazi Germany* (London: Allen Lane, 2016)

Paley, Dawn, *Drug War Capitalism* (Oakland, CA: AK Press, 2014)

Pinchbeck, Daniel, *Breaking Open the Head: A Visionary Journey from Cynicism to Shamanism* (London: Flamingo, 2003)

Pollan, Michael, *How to Change Your Mind: What the New Science of Psychedelics Teaches Us About Consciousness, Dying, Addiction, Depression and Transcendence* (New York, NY: Penguin Press, 2018)

Pollan, Michael, *This is Your Mind on Plants*: *Opium, Caffeine, Mescaline* (London: Allen Lane, 2021)

Power, Mike, *Drugs 2.0: The Web Revolution That's Changing the Way the World Gets High* (London: Portobello, 2013)

Rolles, Steve, *Legalizing Drugs: The Key to Ending the Drug War* (Oxford: New Internationalist, 2017)

Shapiro, Harry, *Fierce Chemistry: A History of UK Drug Wars* (Stroud: Amberley Publishing, 2021)

Smith, Benjamin, *The Dope: The Real History of the Mexican Drug Trade* (London: Penguin, 2021)

Thompson, Hunter S. *Fear and Loathing in Las Vegas* (New York, NY: Random House, 1971)

Webb, Gary, *Dark Alliance: The CIA, the Contras and the Crack Cocaine Explosion* (New York, NY: Seven Stories, 1998)

Wolfe, Tom, *The Electric Kool-Aid Acid Test* (New York, NY: Picador, 1968)

Wood, Philip, *History Under the Influence: Governing on Drugs* (Scotts Valley, CA: CreateSpace, 2015)

Woods, Neil and J. S. Rafaeli, *Drug Wars: The Terrifying Inside Story of Britain's Drug Trade* (London: Ebury, 2018)

Woods, Neil, *Good Cop, Bad War: My Life Undercover inside Britain's Biggest Drugs Gangs* (London: Ebury, 2016)

Picture Credits

Every effort has been made to locate and credit copyright holders of the material reproduced in this book. The author and publisher apologise for any omissions or errors which can be corrected in future editions.

a=above, b=below, c=centre, l=left, r=right

64r Yasuyoshi Chiba/AFP via Getty Images

65 Elena Chernyshova/Bloomberg via Getty Images

66–7 Camilo Freedman/SOPA Images/LightRocket via Getty Images

68 David Pollack/Corbis via Getty Images

69l Dennis Hallinan/Getty Images

69r Ben Martin/Getty Images

70a Mark Reinstein/Corbis via Getty Images

70b AFP via Getty Images

71 Stephan Gladieu/Getty Images

72–3 Andrew Lichtenstein/Corbis via Getty Images

74 Pedro Pardo/AFP via Getty Images

75a Cavan Images/Alamy Stock Photo

75b Pedro Pardo/AFP via Getty Images

76 Eric Vandeville/Gamma-Rapho via Getty Images

77 STR/AFP via Getty Images

78 Susana Gonzalez/Bloomberg via Getty Images

79a Diana Walker/Getty Images

79b ©Bill Gentile/Corbis via Getty Images

80 Evans/Three Lions/Getty Images

81a AP/Shutterstock

81b Orjan F. Ellingvag/Dagbladet/Corbis via Getty Images

82 Raul Arboleda/AFP via Getty Images

83–4 Luis Robayo/AFP via Getty Images

85 Pedro Pardo/AFP via Getty Images

86 Bruce Taylor/New Hampshire State Police Forensic Laboratory

87 Paula Bronstein/Getty Images

88a Robert Nickelsberg/Getty Images

88b Bilal Guler/Anadolu Agency via Getty Images

89 Darren Cullen (spelling mistakescostlives.com)

90 Sean Gallup/Getty Images

91a AFP via Getty Images

91b Francis R Malasig/EPA/Shutterstock

92 Zeke Jacobs/NurPhoto via Getty Images

93 Thames & Hudson

94 Linda Davidson/*The Washington Post* via Getty Images

95 Reuters/Alamy Stock Photo

96 Patrick Smith/Getty Images

97 123rf

98 Alex Wong/Getty Images

99 Contraband Collection/Alamy Stock Photo

100a Orlando Sierra/AFP via Getty Images

100b Mauro Pimentel/AFP via Getty Images

101a Reuters/Alamy Stock Photo

101b Stan Honda/AFP via Getty Images

102–3 David Mcnew/AFP via Getty Images

104 Bryan Steffy/Getty Images

105 Everynight Images/Alamy Stock Photo

106 Raul Arboleda/AFP via Getty Images

107 Thames & Hudson

108 Jonathan Nackstrand/AFP via Getty Images

109a In Pictures Ltd/Corbis via Getty Images

109b Idealink Photography/Alamy Stock Photo

110 John van Hasselt/Sygma via Getty Images

111 Canadian Press/Shutterstock

112l César Maxit/Decriminalize Nature DC

112r Decriminalize Nature Minneapolis, Psychedelic Society of Minnesota

113 Desiree Martin/AFP via Getty Images

114a Cole Burston/Bloomberg via Getty Images

114b Ben Nelms/Bloomberg via Getty Images

115 Gregory Rec/Portland Press Herald via Getty Images

116 David Paul Morris/Bloomberg via Getty Images

117 Transform Drug Policy Foundation (www.transformdrugs.org) & Halo media 2020

118a Roger Cremers/Bloomberg via Getty Images

118b Jochen Tack/Alamy Stock Photo

119l Thames & Hudson

119r Brynn Anderson/AP/Shutterstock

120l Lynsey Addario/Getty Images

120r Lars Hagberg/AFP via Getty Images

121 Albin Lohr-Jones/Pacific Press/LightRocket via Getty Images

122 Steve Russell/Toronto Star via Getty Images

123 Jeff J Mitchell/Getty Images

124 KnowYourStuffNZ

125 protestkit.eu

126 Rungroj Yongrit/EPA/Shutterstock

127a Paula Bronstein/Getty Images

127b Matthew James/Alamy Stock Photo

128–9 Phil Dent/Redferns

130 Fabio Vieira/FotoRua/NurPhoto via Getty Images

131 Mikhail Japaridze/TASS via Getty Images

132 Andrew Lichtenstein/Corbis via Getty Images

133 Alaister Russell/Sowetan/Gallo Images/Getty Images

134l © Fitzwilliam Museum/Bridgeman Images

134r Chatto and Windus, 1954/Private Collection

135 Rick Colls/Shutterstock

Index

Acknowledgments:
A heartfelt thanks to my loving parents Nick and Mandy for everything, and to my brother, Rory. To my aunt and uncle, Judy and Dave, and all of my family. To Becky Gardiner, Terry Kirby, and all of my former classmates and teachers at Goldsmiths; plus Concordia and Royal Holloway. To all of my editors at the *Guardian*, the *Observer*, *Vice*, *Leafly*, *Lucid News* and all the newspapers and magazines that have kindly published my work. To everyone at *The Link* in Montreal, who gave me my first gig and helped teach me to write news. To Steve Rolles from Transform and Niamh Eastwood at Release for their feedback. To Jane Laing, Isabel Jessop, Phoebe Lindsley, Tristan de Lancey and everyone at Thames & Hudson for their incredible work. Lastly, to my dogs Candela and Alma, who bring me so much joy and comfort.

First published in the United Kingdom in 2022 by Thames & Hudson Ltd, 181A High Holborn, London WC1V 7QX

First published in the United States of America in 2022 by Thames & Hudson Inc., 500 Fifth Avenue, New York, New York 10110

Should All Drugs Be Legalized? © 2022 Thames & Hudson Ltd, London

Text © 2022 Mattha Busby

For image copyright information, see pp. 138–39

British Library Cataloguing-in-Publication Data
A catalogue record for this book is available from the British Library

Library of Congress Control Number 2021943175

ISBN 978-0-500-29568-7

Printed and bound in Slovenia by DZS Grafik

FSC MIX Paper from responsible sources FSC® C112556 www.fsc.org